AMY FOSTER

AMY FOSTER

SCREENPLAY AND INTRODUCTION BY
TIM WILLOCKS

THE SHORT STORY "AMY FOSTER" BY
JOSEPH CONRAD

AFTERWORD WITH
BEEBAN KIDRON
AND ## FRED SCHEPISI

SCEPTRE

First published in Great Britain in 1998 by Hodder and Stoughton
A division of Hodder Headline PLC

A Sceptre paperback

10 9 8 7 6 5 4 3 2 1

A CIP catalogue record for this title is available from
the British Library.

ISBN 0 340 73843 X

Printed and bound in Great Britain by
Mackays of Chatham PLC, Chatham, Kent

Hodder and Stoughton
A division of Hodder Headline plc
338 Euston Road
London NW1 3BH

CONTENTS

INTRODUCTION

BY TIM WILLOCKS

I began writing (mostly Westerns and war stories) as a boy, when there was no distinction in my imagination between literature and movies and reenacting the battle of Rourke's Drift on the moors with my friends. When I was fifteen years old I stopped writing for about fifteen years while I pursued a medical career, but during that time—with no thought of ever taking an active part in the arts—I continued to be a passionate reader, viewer, and listener. In a way I never did construct any emotional boundaries between the different art forms and so when, having published my first novel, I started to write screenplays, it seemed no more than a natural extension of my broader love of stories.

That said, I agree with Pinter and Shaffer that the screenplay is the most technically and intellectually exacting of all forms of writing. That is part of the screenplay's addictive quality. It demands intense architectural rigor, an acute awareness of the huge contributions that all the other creative artists (and I do include producers) will make to the film, and a willingness, like the Birdman of Alcatraz, to find freedom of expression within a cage. All the qualities that make writing screenplays infuriating are those that make them a compulsion and a joy. Although they do not yet—and maybe never will—enjoy the prestige of the novel, the stage play, or the poem, I believe screenplays are in every sense the equal of their more revered brethren. Ezra Pound defined "beauty" as "aptness to purpose"; hence the beauty of the V-12 engine or the Brooklyn Bridge as well as of "Paradise Lost." The screenwriter must be a poet *and* an engineer, and a good screenplay is in and of itself, even if it is never produced, a thing of beauty.

I first read Joseph Conrad—*Heart of Darkness, The Secret Agent*—in my late teenage "nihilist period," when anything dark, desolate, and pessimistic held great appeal. But I discovered "Amy Foster" via Bertrand Russell's *Autobiography*, in which he describes "Amy" as one of the most moving stories he had ever read. I read it then, twenty years ago, and it has haunted me ever since. As my own life evolved, my rereadings of the tale changed, too, and I found myself discovering new angles and meanings. The central story—of Yanko—is the classic portrait of a young adventurer whose destiny, like that of many before him, is to be misunderstood, rejected for his differences, and doomed to a tragic death. This is one of the great archetypal themes of both reality and myth and so it will never die, and for a young man this was easy to identify with. When I became a doctor I naturally re-identified with the character of Dr. Kennedy, in a different and, I hope, more profound way, as I dimly comprehended the scale of his devotion and sacrifice in those hard times, the depth of his humanity, "the penetrating power of his mind." To me he became the embodiment of and a monument to the profession of medicine, which the Greeks themselves honored as "the most brilliant of the arts." Both these characters are vividly drawn in Conrad, but it wasn't until I set myself to writing the script that I realized that at the heart of the story—at the heart of Conrad's *telling* of the story—there was a great unexplained mystery.

And that mystery was Amy Foster herself. In the story that bears her name she is virtually invisible.

The story is one of the most beautifully written and technically astonishing in the English language, and for a long time I tried to stay absolutely true to Conrad's depiction of characters and events. It simply did not work. As I tried to retell the story from inside the characters themselves, I found that they—and in particular Amy and Yanko—could not live out the story that Conrad had told *in the way that he had told it*. Amy and Yanko denied Conrad's version of events. And then I realized that the story is told through the eyes of only one man—Kennedy. Studying the story afresh, I realized that Kennedy was by no means the impartial observer he appeared to be, and so writing the script became like *Rashomon*—trying to see the events through the eyes of all the characters in an attempt to be true to *them*. The idea of "being faithful" to the original in writing my screenplay was, as I now see it, a comforting fantasy, a blanket beneath which to hide. The only possible true fidelity to an author is to leave the original work entirely alone. All art demands a certain degree of arrogance and ruthlessness, and I decided that if Verdi could gut *Macbeth* (and, on the way, turn it into one of the greatest feats of all creation), then I could free myself to retell "Amy Foster." So I let Conrad spin in his grave and asked the characters themselves to tell me a different version of what happened.

In fact, I drew all the answers from the story itself. The "Amy" that Conrad/Kennedy gives us is rather ugly and, to put it kindly, educationally subnormal. Yet the only evidence we have of this is Kennedy's opinion: "It's enough to look at those slow brown eyes to know the inertness of her mind." Well, it's *not* enough. As we all know, there are several Nobel Prize winners who at some time in their lives endured just such assessments of their minds on the basis of just such crude and unsubstantiated "evidence," and there are many millions more who have been enslaved, tortured, and exterminated on similar bases. So I searched for further evidence of her stupidity. This amounts to little more than the fact that "she had never been heard to express dislike for a single human being and was tender to every living creature." Clearly an idiot, then. And for a man of Kennedy's generation it did not help her case that she was a woman, a category at that time deemed to lack even the intelligence to vote, and that she was of the lowest social order—an unskilled working-class wage-slave—to boot. It seemed to me, then, that like the multitudes before and since who have been unjustly condemned on the basis of race, gender, creed, and eye-color, this was enough, in Kennedy/Conrad's mind, to relegate Amy to the category of simpleton. And on the subject of the perception of "ugliness" or "beauty," I should say that there isn't a supermodel alive today who would have got a job advertising laundry detergent, let alone high-fashion, even twenty years ago; so Kennedy's account of her physical appearance is hardly reliable either.

Even so, what is the evidence for disagreeing with him?

For a start, tenderness and pity are gifts that I associate more with wisdom and sensitivity than with cretinism. More importantly, she immediately recognizes that Yanko is, even if nothing else, a fellow human being; *everyone else* sees only a sub-human beast. Whose "intelligence" would you rather be at the mercy of? Not only that, she has the sense to realize that, man or beast, he is in wretched shape and needs food and water. She acts decisively, courageously, and in open defiance of those who are not merely her "bosses" but, literally, her lords (or ladies) and masters. She continues this defiance, even when "every old woman in the village was up in arms." She conducts her duties as a servant (the laboriousness and multiplicity of which would undoubtedly crush most of us today) with total competence. And—at the beginning and end of the story—she appears to be a perfectly adequate single mother living an independent life—no mean feat today, and something of a heroic achievement, I would say, amidst the social brutality of the late nineteenth century. So the *facts* Conrad gives us about Amy are actually at odds with his *opinion* of her.

But for me the most compelling evidence that Amy is not the ugly, slow-minded simpleton that Conrad would have us believe is Yanko himself. About this man Conrad has no doubts—he is very good-looking, long-limbed, musical, quick-witted, graceful, sensitive, and intelligent (he learns an entirely alien language with startling speed). We are asked to believe that this man is so grateful that Amy Foster gave him a piece of bread that he falls wildly in love with her—and not just any love but "love as the Ancients knew it"—and asks her to marry him. I would suggest that a love of this intensity, in any human being, in any culture, at any time in history, must be built on something rather deeper than gratitude. One can, after all, just say "Thank you." So Yanko, at least, saw something in Amy not only "to fall in love with," but through which he could sustain his love despite violence, hatred, hell and high water. Kennedy's "explanation" of this is, frankly, racist: "Perhaps amongst types so different from what he had ever seen, he had not the power to judge"; i.e., "because he's a foreigner he can't recognize a dog when he sees one." So neither Conrad nor Kennedy gives us any real understanding at all of the love story. Amy, as they would have it, would fall in love with "a toad in difficulties," given the chance; but by Yanko's love for Amy they are entirely bewildered.

So this is the mystery of Conrad's "Amy Foster": Who is Amy Foster and why does Yanko love her?

I decided to solve this by investigating the clues that Conrad gives to her possible hidden personality, and by extrapolating from his hasty descriptions of their courtship to discover something that would justify their great love. Conrad gives Amy a dysfunctional family—he refers obliquely to her own parents' scandalous marriage. This presented me with an opportunity both to give Amy a dramatic backstory and, at the same time, to explain psychologically why she is socially withdrawn and perceived as strange. Modern psychology recognizes that social withdrawal and educational underachievement are classic defenses to a painful or traumatic family milieu. Such children are often scapegoated, and they not uncommonly invent for themselves an alternative world, free of pain and strife, in which they can live and express themselves without judgment or humiliation. Indeed, many famous creative personalities took this route in their own childhoods, and it is a commonplace that such people tend to be outsiders or oddballs in some way. So I used Conrad's clues—the family, Amy's strangeness—to construct in more detail her life story and her secret world. This made both her and her parents much richer characters, and made it possible to believe in Yanko's love for her.

It also made Kennedy much more central to the drama. Instead of being the objective observer he believes himself to be, he is revealed as the third corner of the dramatic triangle. In many ways the core of the story is Kennedy's own journey—through his great debate with Miss Swaffer—of self-discovery and enlightenment. He is a man of outstanding wisdom and compassion, and yet the depth of his own feelings contaminates his objectivity and leads him into the cruel error of misjudging Amy Foster. One of the most powerful impulses for me in translating the story was the moment in the original when Kennedy suggests that Yanko has vanished forever from Amy's brain. Every time I read this I wanted to scream "How can you say that?" From a man of such intelligence it is a preposterous suggestion. And I still don't know what was in Conrad's mind—after all, he even has Amy name her child after Yanko!

So trying to answer that question—"How could such an intelligent man make such a stupid statement?"—opened up the character to fascinating psychological detective work.

Only raw emotion can blind intellect to that degree, and so I deduced that Kennedy was himself so deeply moved by Yanko's fate that he had to defend himself from his grief by blaming Amy. He could not blame himself, and despite his profession, whose bread and butter is blameless tragedy, he was too involved in this particular "case" to take the philosophical view in which he normally prided himself and which he exemplifies with such grace elsewhere. Kennedy too, then, became a much richer, multi-dimensional character; indeed, his is the most complex journey in the film. In the story Kennedy is God-like, and his view goes unquestioned. In the film he discovers that he is, after all, only a man, and in so doing redeems himself and achieves an incomparably greater dignity.

And although Conrad's story was mainly about Yanko, it actually left *his* story untold as well, because if we know so little about the love of his life, we cannot really know very much about him either. This is the nature of love, in life as in literature: one must know both lovers in order to truly know either of them. We all fall in love in order to discover our own deepest self, and that great discovery is the greatest gift that lovers make to each other.

It struck me that "Amy Foster" was one of the greatest love stories ever told, except that the love story itself had been left out. Conrad, like Kennedy, was a man of his time, and it seems that he neither understood Amy's character nor especially cared to do so. Throughout his work as a whole, women are few and sparsely written. And why should they not be? Conrad had other concerns and preoccupations and gave us some of the greatest literature in English, despite it being his third language. So it would be foolish and ungracious to say this was a failing in his magnificent work. Certainly I would never suggest that the film was in any way "better" than the story; it is simply another telling of the same tale, and such "other tellings" have a noble history stretching from Homer himself to Martin Scorcese.

This web of deep psychological mysteries, then, was what sustained my interest in the screenplay. *All* the parts as written were, I believe, difficult, and demanded exceptional insight and invention from the filmmakers. When I saw the film, I was enormously moved and astonished to discover that all these characters—whom I thought I had known so well—were in fact even deeper, more complex, and more extraordinary than I myself had imagined. Every line, every scene, every vista hit me as something new, something startling. It was as if I was experiencing the story for the very first time. The sheer beauty of the film and its raw emotional power swept over me like a tidal wave. And it brought home to me that the script is only the map, not the territory. Being taken into that territory by the filmmakers made me feel like Columbus—he knew the New World was there, but had no idea how beautiful, how majestic, how infinitely detailed it actually was.

Finally, I must stress that although the screenplay is credited to me it was in truth written by many people. Every member of the crew in some way "rewrote" it with their own creativity and expertise, but in particular Beeban Kidron and Christy Prunier put innumerable suggestions, insights, ideas, and major plot points into the script and the characters that entirely transformed what I had originally written. If the script is of some worth, then much of the credit goes to them rather than to me, and I am greatly in their debt. I am also indebted to the many people I've known in my life who unknowingly contributed to the richness of the characters. In a way, I know all of the real-life equivalents. And I'd like to acknowledge a special debt to a lifelong friend and mentor, Bodan Daszak—to me, "Uncle Bob."

Bob was Ukrainian. He taught me how to play chess, poker, and the guitar; how to build giant kites from wood and brown wrapping paper; and many, many other things. When he was thirteen years old, at the close of World War II, his father understood that peace for the Ukraine meant a new Stalinist terror, so he told Bob to leave and try to make his way to freedom. Bob, alone and still a boy, *walked* from the Ukraine—across war-ravaged Hungary and Yugoslavia—to Italy, and finally made his way to the North of England, where he made his family and his home. Bob's wife, Ruth, was my godmother, so all my life I absorbed his love of music and the dance, his way with English, his robust and emotional masculinity, his moments of distant melancholy. There is a lot of Bob in Yanko. Bob died last year, before filming started, but I like to think that in some small way, my writing of the character of Yanko is my memorial to Bob Daszak and his incomparable race.

The experience of "Amy Foster" has shown me the true glory of film-making: the way that many different human minds and spirits are drawn together and merge into the one seamless whole of the film. The audience then extends that wholeness. I like to think that this film in particular forms a great human chain throughout time and space. From the emigrants and country-folk, who in reality suffered and lived so heroically and whose lives are, I hope, honored by this film; through Joseph Conrad and Bertrand Russell and Bob Daszak; to us who have made the movie; and beyond to those who will watch it now and in time to come, this story brings people together—past, present, and future—into a celebration of our shared humanity and of our eternal hope and faith: that love can indeed triumph over death.

<u>Amy Foster</u>

Screenplay by
Tim Willocks

Based on the short story "Amy Foster" by
Joseph Conrad

NOTE ON THE PUBLISHED SCRIPT

The script as published does not correspond exactly to the final film. *Amy Foster* went through many drafts in pre-production. What follows is the script as it was shortly before filming began. Changes were made during filming, most in post-production as the film emerged. Some cuts simply made the film flow better and some additions were absolutely necessary for clarity. But many are double-edged — while improving one aspect of the film they intrude upon another.

In the context of this publication, we thought it more interesting to provide this slightly earlier draft rather than a transcription of the film. The asterisks indicate scene changes and omissions made after filming began.

— Beeban Kidron

1   EXT. TALFOURD HILL - EASTBAY. EVENING.   1

The foaming splendour of a limitless SEA.

Enclosing it in a vast and regular sweep -- are miles of
barren SHINGLE BEACH. Beyond the rocky headland stands a
lighthouse; and beyond that - above the far-flung western
horizon - a bank of clouds are purple-red in the setting sun.

Sweeping around across the landscape -- a shadowed VALLEY: a
rugged green trough of moors and hedges. Then: the slope of a
steep HILL, halfway up which stands a small, isolated
cottage. Finally --

A WOMAN'S FACE:

She is young. Her features are plain but striking; her hair
is drawn into a tight knot at the back of her head. In her
eyes is a sense of willful self-containment - as if she
carries all that she needs deep within herself.

This is AMY FOSTER.

                    CHILD'S VOICE
                    (O.S.)
          The sea!

Amy looks down: a LITTLE BOY stands by her side. He's three
years old; black hair; his eyes are dark and fearless. His
arm points out to sea.

                    BOY
          The sea!

                    AMY
          Yes, the sea.That is where you came from.

The boy doesn't understand - but smiles nonetheless. Amy
smiles too - yet there is also a haunted sadness in her eyes.
She turns as she hears, then sees:

The clatter of wheels and hooves. Racing urgently along the
cliff road is a two-wheeled CART. The driver waves his whip.

Amy takes the boy's hand and starts towards the road.

The driver hauls his panting horse to a halt by Amy and her
boy . He's a gaunt old man of eighty-five -- with lank grey
hair and austere, phlegmatic features.

This is MR. SWAFFER.

                                        (CONTINUED)

1   CONTINUED: 1

                              SWAFFER
                    Amy? The daughter's taken a turn. She
                    asked for you.

Without fuss or hesitation Amy lifts the boy up onto the seat
beside Swaffer.

                              SWAFFER
                    I've sent a man to fetch Doctor Kennedy.

Amy - about to climb up herself - hesitates. The name
provokes difficult feelings -- but only for an instant. She
swings onto the seat, takes the boy on her lap.

The cart swings in a tight U and clatters down the hill.

2   EXT. COLEBROOK VILLAGE. EVENING.   2

A small village defended from the sea by a great, curving
wall and dominated by a fine Gothic church spire. A few
villagers walk the main street. Heads turn as --

A Phaeton carriage - more elegant than Swaffer's cart and
drawn by two horses - rumbles down the cobbles.

The driver is hatless and dressed as a gentleman. His
features are distinguished, intelligent, yet rugged. His eyes
are profound yet intense, with the possibility of fierceness
in the brows.

This is DOCTOR JAMES KENNEDY.

Kennedy cracks his whip. The horses pick up speed.

3   EXT. SWAFFER'S FARM. EVENING.   3

A fine, rambling greystone farmhouse.

Swaffer sits on the porch steps, sucking on a dry long-
stemmed pipe. He watches -

The BOY playing in the garden. Swaffer stands up as:

KENNEDY races into the yard and pulls up.

Kennedy strides towards Swaffer. They shake hands.

                              KENNEDY
                    Swaffer.

                              SWAFFER
                    Appreciate your coming so prompt, Doctor.

Kennedy makes as if to brush this off, then reacts, surprised
- a dark, troubled, surprise - as he sees:

                                                            (CONTINUED)

3   CONTINUED: 3

The BOY tottering towards them.

Kennedy - suddenly haunted. He shoots Swaffer a glance.

                    SWAFFER
          Amy's indoors.

                    KENNEDY
          With Miss Swaffer?

                    SWAFFER
          The daughter says Amy is a strength to
          her.

Kennedy's muted anger is then assailed by --

The BOY - who stops and looks up at Kennedy uncertainly.

Kennedy: his haunted eyes. He crouches down.

                    KENNEDY
          What a fine figure of a man you are
          becoming.

Kennedy musters a smile. The Boy hides behind Swaffer.

Kennedy stands, collects himself. He strides to the house.

As Kennedy opens the door he notices --

A weathered chess table on the porch nearby.

Kennedy blinks. He goes into the house.

4   INT. SWAFFER'S HOUSE. NIGHT.   4

The house is cool and dark, austerely decorated.

At one end of a corridor is a door. In an alcove stands a
19th century wheelchair Kennedy walks towards the door.

5   INT. MISS SWAFFER'S ROOM. EVENING.   5

A large bedroom, heavy dark woods, lace curtains.

In bed lies MISS SWAFFER - woman of forty-seven with steady
grey eyes. Her face is the colour of candle wax, and sheened
with sweat. The sheet below her waist is pulled back to
reveal her legs beneath her nightgown.

AMY FOSTER takes a gauze dressing and gently applies it to --

A large black-edged ulcer infiltrating her calf and shin.

There is a sharp rap at the door. Amy turns as --

                                                    (CONTINUED)

5   CONTINUED: 5

         The door opens and Kennedy enters. Their eyes meet.

         Kennedy leaves the door open for her.

                          KENNEDY
                 Thank you for your care, Amy. You will
                 not be needed further.

                          AMY
                 If you please, sir, I intended to stay
                 with Miss Swaffer through the night.

                          KENNEDY
                 If I consider it necessary, I will stay.

         This rebuke cuts Amy deeply - but she conceals it. She looks
         at --

         Miss Swaffer - who, despite her fever, has observed all this
         with steady eyes.

                          MISS SWAFFER
                 Leave the doctor to attend me, Amy. And
                 thank you.

         Cut down she curtsies briefly to Miss Swaffer - then walks
         out without looking at Kennedy.

         The door closes behind her.

6   INT. SWAFFER'S HOUSE - THE CORRIDOR. EVENING.   6

         Amy stands alone in the corridor for a moment. She is close
         to tears. Then - in almost an instant - all the emotion
         vanishes inside her. Her face is impassive. She walks away.

7   INT. MISS SWAFFER'S BEDROOM. EVENING.   7

         Miss Swaffer has her head turned to one side on the pillow -
         as if in shame. The sheet is pulled back from her legs.

         Infiltrating her calf and shin is -- a large, raw,
         suppurating ulcer. Kennedy removes the gauze dressing.

         Kennedy unpacks bottles and surgical instruments from his bag
         on a table under the window. He looks up through the window
         and sees:

         AMY climbing back onto Swaffer's cart with her boy.

         Kennedy: troubled. He turns back to his instruments. Then --

                          MISS SWAFFER
                          (O.S.)
                 Your cruelty was unnecessary, Doctor.

                                                         (CONTINUED)

Kennedy turns - too astonished to be affronted. Miss
Swaffer's eyes meet his.

> MISS SWAFFER
> Do you too consider her a simpleton?

Kennedy brings over a tray of instruments and prepares to
debride the wound.

> KENNEDY
> It is not my purpose to consider Amy
> Foster at all. You risk gangrene of the
> blood. I must cut away the poisoned flesh
> or it will take you with it before the
> night is out. Why wasn't I called sooner?

Miss Swaffer again turns her head away.

> MISS SWAFFER
> I wouldn't let them.

> KENNEDY
> My God. Shame is all well and good for
> the living - but precious little use to
> the dead.

> MISS SWAFFER
> For all that you invoke God's name, you
> are not a believing man, are you Doctor
> Kennedy?

> KENNEDY
> Even if I were to believe in so merciless
> a being, I could not worship him.

> MISS SWAFFER
> Then you are alone indeed.

> KENNEDY
> (dismissively)
> You are feverish.

> MISS SWAFFER
> Perhaps that gives me license to be bold.
> Reluctant as you may be to -- consider --
> Amy, it would comfort me to know the tale
> entire.

Kennedy looks at her sharply - as if a door has opened he
would rather not enter. He pretends not to understand.

> MISS SWAFFER
> Amy will not speak of him either. If I am
> to die --

(CONTINUED)

7   CONTINUED: 7

                         KENNEDY
                You will not die. I will not permit it.

                         MISS SWAFFER
                Then perhaps it will ease my fever. And
                yours too.

Kennedy looks into her eyes - and cannot defy their wisdom.

                         KENNEDY
                I dare say no one person knows the tale
                entire. But perhaps I know more than
                most. More than most.

Kennedy turns to her wound - his expertise concentrated on
his work as he talks. A strain of stirring East European
music - a folk dance - arises.

                         KENNEDY
                He was a highlander - a 'mountaineer' -
                from a remote corner of the Carpathian
                Mountains.

8   EXT. THE CARPATHIAN MOUNTAINS - THE UKRAINE. LATE EVENING.   8

Moonlight and stars illuminate the crags of a rugged mountain
range. The music gets louder as we see --

A rough stone longhouse and timber barn perch at one end of a
high meadow. Yellow light spills from the open door of the
barn - along with music and voices.

9   INT. THE BARN. NIGHT.   9

A great, passionate, stomping, party shakes the barn to its
rafters. Trestles of food, kegs, jugs of wine. A gathering of
the clan. Everywhere: the work- and weather-worn faces of a
hardy race - men and women, old and young - are animated with
both the sadness and the joy of a great valediction.

And there is dancing. Oh yes. On a pair of wagons placed end
to end THE BAND - accordian, fiddler, mandolin, balalaika,
some tinny brass, bass - play their hearts out for --

The DANCERS -- whirling and turning and gyrating across the
dusty wooden floor. As the music - full-blooded and dark -
gets steadily faster, more passionate, the dancers - men and
women - drop out one by one and retreat - sweating and
smiling - to the audience fringing the arena. One of the ex-
dancers is a raw-boned, bandy legged man with white hair,
vigorous despite his years. This is NIKOLAS.

A hand slaps him on the back and Nikolas accepts, grabs the
proferred mug of wine, and drains it in one. He lowers the
mug and points it at the dancers and makes a boast. His
friends jeer and snort. Nikolas turns and sees:

                                                    (CONTINUED)

9   CONTINUED: 9

A woman - a little younger than him, grey-haired, in her best
dress and shoes, red hands clasped before her. This is IRYNA,
his wife. She watches the dancers with sadness in her eyes.
Nikolas puts his arm around her waist.

There are only four couples left on the floor - young men and
women moving from one partner to the other. One of them -
lithe, striking, with long, flowing hair - dances with a
particular light in his eyes, a special nimbleness of step.

This is YANKO.

As he makes a turn he alters course - sashays backwards - and
with a warm, dazzling smile sweeps his arm over and across in
an elegant, graceful bow towards --

Iryna. Her eyes fill with tears. She squeezes the hand around
her waist and presses closer to her husband.

The music changes - subtly at first, then with no-holds-
barred - into something more fierce. Something that reminds
them all that the dance is most fundamentally not the merry-
maker's rite - but the warrior's.

The women leave the floor leaving only the four young men.
They leap and wheel, each his arms doubled across his chest,
dancing at each other rather than with. The crowd, sensing
the excitement, start to clap and stomp their feet in time,
urging them on in what is now a fierce contest. One man
stumbles, catches his balance - but is gone. He joins the
crowd, smiling wryly.

Nikolas, pride in his eyes, unclasps his arm and joins in the
clapping. He nods to Iryna. She claps too.

Another man - crouching low, shooting out his legs - misses
his footing and reels backwards. Arms in the crowd catch him,
laughing, and haul him to his feet before he hits the dust.
There are only two dancers left.

And how they dance - as if their very lives were at issue.
Back and forth, the music and the stomping getting faster,
faster. Yanko's long damp hair whirls and sticks to his face.
His dark eyes flash - re-focusing, instantly, with each spin
of his body on the eyes of his opponent - who is a worthy
antagonist. Their boots raise clouds of dust and straw. Their
sweat flies in scattered drops. Their breath - visible in the
cool night air - snorts through flared nostrils.

Yanko performs a great - impossible - leap-and-twist. He
lands - perfectly.

His opponent cannot refuse the challenge. Another impossible
leap -- but his landing betrays him. A tiny stumble, he
recovers but -- too late.

(CONTINUED)

9   CONTINUED: 9

The crowd roar their verdict and surge forward.

The musicians - exhausted - gratefully lower their
instruments.

Nikolas and Iryna see Yanko disappear amongst the press of
bodies -- then reappear as he is hoisted high onto their
shoulders. He is carried forward to his parents and lowered
down in triumph. Yanko opens his arms and embraces Iryna.

Yanko - his head over Iryna's shoulder, sees Nikolas nod
solemn approval. Yanko smiles. Then he feels Iryna's body
shudder against him. He pulls back, looks into her eyes. She
is crying. For his sake, she musters a smile.

Yanko - moved by her tears, then --

A mug is thrust into his hand. He looks at his father --
receives the blessing of his eyes. Yanko turns to the crowd.
He raises his wine.

                    YANKO
          AMERIKA!

                    THE CROWD
          AMERIKA!

Amidst cheers Yanko downs his wine in one.

10   OMITTED   10*

11   EXT. A RAILWAY TRACK - A BOXCAR. DAY.   11*

A steam engine - Hauling a long string of boxcars pulls in,   *
slows to a wheezing halt. Several small clusters of people   *
stand wailing by the tracks. One of the groups is.   *

YANKO'S FAMILY; Yanko, dressed to travel: a satchel, a bundle   *
at his feet. As the train pulls in his family smother him   *
with tearfull goodbyes and gifts - It's all happening at   *
once.   *

Brother Bodan loops a string of amulets around Yanko's neck.   *

Brother Petr takes from around his own neck -- a silver   *
crucifix. He puts it around Yanko's neck.   *

Iryna presses a small wad of money - he tries to refuse - she   *
forces it into his palm, crying. Yanko hugs her. He shakes   *
hands - hurriedly, one after the other - with his other   *
brothers.   *

Finally - Nikolas looks into Yanko's eyes. They embrace.   *
Yanko turns, with a rumble --   *

The boxcar door slides open to reveal: Half a dozen men   *
sitting with their luggage on the straw.   *

                                              (CONTINUED)

11 CONTINUED: 11

Yanko hauls himself away from his family - all smiling,   *
waving, crying, a few last slaps on the back - and tosses his   *
bundle into the boxcar. As he starts to climb up --   *

A YOUNG MAN holds his hand down towards him and smiles. Yanko   *
takes it and the man hauls him up.   *

                    STEFAN   *
          Yanko!   *

                    YANKO   *
          Stefan!   *

As the train lurches, Stefan gestures as if to say, 'listen   *
to this!'. He speaks - stumblingly - in ENGLISH.   *

                    STEFAN   *
          We are the -- lucky ones!   *

Yanko doesn't even know what it means - but he is impressed -   *
and a little envious. Challenged, he tries --   *

                    YANKO   *
          Weh - re - de lukeewuz.   *

Stefan laughs and claps him on the back. Yanko grins. The   *
grin fades into sadness as he turns and sees: *

His family - waving - by the track as the train pulls away.   *
Yanko's eyes are drawn to those of--   *

Nikolas - Grizzled, sad, immensely proud. Over the scenes of   *
Yanko's departure we hear Nikolas's VOICE - as if these are   *
the unspoken words that pass between them: *

                    NIKOLAS'S VOICE   *
          The lust of the wanderer is in your blood -   *
          and you must search for your true gold.   *

YANKO - framed in the boxcar door, pulling away -- away --   *

                    NIKOLAS'S VOICE   *
          Eat well and say your prayers each day.   *
          Carry yourself like a man, for though we   *
          are not rich, we have never been slaves.   *
          And remember, that whatever God's will may   *
          be, we are proud of you - and you will be with   *
          us, always, in our inmost hearts.   *

The train pulls away into the immense landscapes.   *

12 EXT. THE MOUNTAINS - POLAND. DAY.   12

A stark - beautiful - mountain valley. At first there seems
no sign that man has ever laid his hand on it, then --

                                                        (CONTINUED)

12   CONTINUED: 12

      A plume of black smoke and -- a steam engine labours,
      clanking, into view, hauling behind it a long procession of
      weathered boxcars.

13   EXT. THE STEPPES. SUNSET.   13

      A vast landscape - flat as far as the horizon in every
      direction. The train - dwarfed by the immensity of the plain
      - ploughs towards the setting sun.

13a   EXT. A CITY. DAWN.   13a

      The train approaches the outskirts of a LARGE CITY: smoking
      chimneys, heavy industry, great skeletons of steel and stone.

14   EXT. THE BOXCAR. DAWN.   14

      The train is stopped at a crossroads, the doors shut. One
      door slides open. A slop bucket is dumped at the feet of --

      A crowd of baffled emigrants clustered by the track.

      INSIDE: The floor of the boxcar is now CRAMMED with
      exhausted, filthy men curled upon and amongst each other. The
      foul air hums with flies.

      YANKO, his knees drawn up, his back to the wall, is haggard,
      dirty and weary. His face is covered with days of matted
      growth. The gleam has gone from his eyes. He rises stiffly,
      grabs for his bundle, as --

      Railroad guards bellow, and shove the new emigrants on board.

      Yanko glances at STEFAN: also hungry, tired and filthy. YANKO
      musters a smile and squeezes his arm.

                        YANKO
                We ah th' luki wunz.

      The boxcar door rumbles shut - trapping us inside. The
      interior is now totally - inhumanly - jammed from wall to
      wall with weary men. The train lurches into motion.

15   EXT. A RAILWAY YARD - HAMBURG. DAY.   15

      Grey skies. Rain. The train pulls into a long platform. As it
      wheezes to a halt we rise above to take an overhead view of
      the boxcars as --

      The DOORS rumble open and a great mass of bone-weary humanity
      spills out onto the platform.

16   INT. YANKO'S BOXCAR. DAY.   16

      Yanko blinks as light floods the dim, foetid interior. His
      beard is now full, and matted with filth. He glances down at
      a face, snoring on his shoulder. It's Stefan.

                                                        (CONTINUED)

16   CONTINUED: 16

          Yanko is too exhausted for emotion. He hears shouts -- barely
          bothers to turn. Then he realizes that there is a movement
          amongst them. He cranes his head, sees:

          MEN jumping from the doors.

          Yanko - hardly daring to hope - shakes Stefan awake.

17   EXT. YANKO'S BOXCAR. DAY.   17

          YANKO passes two bundles down to STEFAN and jumps out. They
          exchange a look: their spirits rising again. They hoist their
          bundles and follow the crowd towards --

18   EXT. THE RIVER ELBE. DAY.   18

          The emigrants are funnelled like cattle down a passageway
          between rusting corrugated iron walls. The rain beats down.
          Amongst the crowd are many women and children. The passageway
          finally opens out onto:

          A harbour alongside a broad river.

          Sullen stewards shout and shove the emigrants towards a
          series of large, low, barges. Yanko and Stefan climb aboard.

19   OMITTED   19*

20   EXT. THE BARGE. NIGHT.   20*

          The barge ploughs down the river.   *

          On the deck: a mass of freezing emigrants huddled together.   *

          Amongst them: Yanko and Stefan. Stefan tugs Yanko's sleeve,   *
          points excitedly. Yanko peers out into the darkness.   *

          Looming ahead in a dim yellow lght is what appears to be a   *
          smooth black wall.   *

                              STEFAN   *
                     Amerika! Yes? Amerika?   *

          Shouts and hurly burly. The barge bumps into a wall.   *

          Yanko looks up with awe: *

          The towering MASTS and RIGGING of A SAILING SHIP. LADDERS   *
          tumble towards the barge's deck.   *

21   EXT. THE SAILING SHIP. NIGHT.   21

          Like harried rats the emigrants climb the precarious ladders. *

          As Yanko clears the gunwale a dour SEAMEN gives Yanko a shove   *
          towards a line of people. In the distance he sees -- Stefan.   *

                                                            (CONTINUED)

21   CONTINUED: 21

                              YANKO   *
                    Stefan!   *

Stefan turns, catches sight of Yanko, beckons to him.   *

Yanko tries to step out of line but the seaman curses at him   *
and shoves him roughly back. With a sudden flash of dark   *
anger Yanko turns on him, raising his fist. The seaman takes   *
a step back, afraid; then to save face: *

                              SEAMAN   *
                    Just get down below, yer bleeding yahoo.   *

Yanko turns to see: Stefan disappear through a door -- which   *
is slammed shut behind him.   *

Amongst surly shouts, shoving hands and dour faces, YANKO   *
follows his own line towards A SECOND DOOR further aft of   *
him.   *

22   INT. THE SHIP - THE 'TWEEN DECKS. NIGHT.   22

YANKO reaches the foot of a ladder and turns to see:

THE 'TWEEN DECKS: a large, damp, foetid space with a low
timber roof and stacked with narrow bunks. DRIPPING WATER.
CREAKING WALLS. The ship LURCHES from side to side. The
appalling space teems with bewildered emigrants. The air
rings with the cries of children, mothers both shouting and
comforting, men arguing over bunks.

Yanko's face reveals his horror of this place. Amidst the
babble he hears --

                              1st MAN   *
                    To America? Five, six weeks. More if   *
                    there is no wind.   *

Yanko, trying to keep his spirits up - turns to a rack of   *
three bunks right next to the ladder. He stops as he finds: *

A tiny, white, bewildered FACE staring at him from the top   *
bunk. It's a little girl. Her eyes stare at him.   *

Yanko smiles at her with reassurance he doesn't really feel.

The girl's expression doesn't change.   *

On impulse Yanko takes the SILVER CRUCIFIX from around his   *
neck and loops it over the little girls head. She touches it,   *
shyly, doesn't speak.   *

Yanko smiles and climbs into the middle bunk. His legs are   *
too long, the bunk to narrow. His head turns as: *

The door in the roof above is SLAMMED SHUT.

                                                        (CONTINUED)

13.

22   CONTINUED: 22

       YANKO stares at the timbers inches away from his face.

                                                                 FADE TO

23   INT. MISS SWAFFER'S ROOM. NIGHT.   23

       Kennedy - almost gagging at the smell - works on Miss
       Swaffer's leg. He cuts away a strip of necrotic flesh with
       scalpel and tweezers and drops it into a bowl.

                         MISS SWAFFER
                At least he had his dream for company.

                         KENNEDY
                Yes. And found himself a nightmare.

                         MISS SWAFFER
                Until he met Amy Foster.

                         KENNEDY
                Fate is both inscrutable and without
                mercy, Miss Swaffer.

                         MISS SWAFFER
                Your determination to blame Amy is
                bedfellow to those who say that she
                herself brought the storm that night.

       Kennedy is affronted.

                         KENNEDY
                You insult me, Miss Swaffer. 'Witchcraft'
                and other such despicable superstitions
                are abhorrent to me.

                         MISS SWAFFER
                Even so, the storm came.

       Kennedy turns back to his work, his eyes haunted.

                         KENNEDY
                Yes. Yes, indeed.

24   EXT. A CLIFF BY THE SEA. SUNDOWN.   24

       The waves roll up the beach and fall back short of the cliff
       in which gapes -- the dark, narrow entrance to a CAVE.

       By the entrance lie -- a pair of boots and a grey hat.

       From the darkness of the cave emerges: AMY FOSTER.

       She is BAREFOOT and her hair is wet through, stuck to her
       cheek. Her dress clings to her damp skin. Her FACE is
       radiant. Amy stops in the doorway. She runs her hands through
       her hair, squeezing out the water. Halfway through the
       movement, head tilted, she stops, her eyes fixed on --

                                                        (CONTINUED)

24   CONTINUED: 24

        The rolling immensity of THE SEA. Barely audible: a distant
        roll of thunder.

        AMY throws her hair back. She covers the narrow cave entrance
        with a sheaf of weather-bleached brushwood.

25   EXT. THE FIELDS. SUNSET.   25

        Framed in the melancholy counterscarps of the steeply rising
        ground is AMY . Behind her: the last slivered rim of the sun
        clings to the horizon.

        AMY walks across a harrowed field. Bare trees. Brown earth. A
        snowless winter landscape.

        AMY walks down the hill. In the sky looms a dark bank of
        storm clouds. THUNDER peals out across the twilit fields.
        Then: a BOLT of lightning.

        AMY'S FACE: as drops of rain start to strike her cheeks.

26   EXT. THE COLEBROOK ROAD. EVENING.   26

        In the distance: the light of a floating buoy blinks in the
        shadowy bay. A blast of lighting briefly illuminates a SHIP
        sailing in from the open sea towards the buoy.

        ON THE ROAD: KENNEDY sits on his stationary carriage,
        buttoning up his oilskin coat. He stops as something catches
        his eye:

        ON THE HILL: a figure is dancing in the rain.

        It's AMY FOSTER. She stands arms spread wide, and turns in a
        slow - sensuous - circle. Her feet are bare. Her clothes are
        drenched through. Her long wet hair flies in the wind. Her
        face and gleaming eyes are turned up to the rain - as if
        riding the heart of the rising tempest. She stops mid turn as
        she sees --

        KENNEDY watching her from the road. He looks mystified.

        AMY stares back at him, without blinking.

        Kennedy snaps the reins and pulls away.

27   EXT. NEW BARNS FARM - THE YARD. NIGHT.   27

        A MAELSTROM of howling wind and rain. Barking dogs. From the
        stable comes the sound of terrified horses. MR. SMITH stomps
        grimly through the rain calling to men in oilskins who lurch
        about the darkness with lanterns.

                        MR SMITH
                Malcolm! Get the beasts out of there,
                sharp! Put 'em in the back meadow! THE
                MEADOW I SAY!

                                                            (CONTINUED)

27 CONTINUED: 27

A roof slate tumbles crashing to the cobbles.

                    MR SMITH
            And watch yourselves - the Devil's riding
            this wind tonight!

28 EXT. NEW BARNS FARM - THE KITCHEN. NIGHT.   28

MRS. SMITH, a forceful, genteel woman - appears at the door
and calls out across the yard towards:

A room above the milking sheds. The window is dark.

                    MRS. SMITH
        Amy? Amy!

No answer. Mrs. Smith - exasperated - pulls her coat over her
head and dashes out into the rain.

29 INT. AMY'S ROOM. NIGHT.   29

AMY stands close to the window in the dark. The panes rattle
with the force of the rain. The wind howls. AMY seems
entranced by the elemental forces beyond the glass. On an
impulse she unfastens the latch and opens the window. The
gale wrenches it from her grasp like a whip.

The window snaps against its hinge -- the glass shatters.

30 EXT. THE YARD. NIGHT.   30

SMITH looks up as a shower of glass falls to the cobbles.

                    SMITH
            What the bloody hell?

31 INT. AMY'S ROOM. NIGHT.   31

AMY stands at the open window as the driving wind lashes her
face with rain. Exhilarated - intoxicated by the wild untamed
spirit of the storm - she shuts her eyes.

                    MRS. SMITH
        AMY!

AMY wheels: her joy vanishes. Her face closes. Mrs. Smith -
wet - rushes past and reaches out to grab the window. Below:

                    MR SMITH
            Jesus, Mary and Joseph!

Mrs. Smith hauls the broken window shut and fastens it.

                    MRS. SMITH
            Now you have him blaspheming, you stupid,
            stupid girl! Don t you think we have
            enough to deal with? And why don't you
            have the light on?

                                            (CONTINUED)

31 CONTINUED: 31

    AMY doesn't reply. Mrs. Smith gives up: anger is futile.

                    MRS. SMITH
            Then go and make Mr. Smith some good
            strong tea. Lord knows what he'll have to
            say about this.

    AMY curtsies and goes to the door.

32 EXT. THE ENGLISH CHANNEL. NIGHT.   32

    The emigrant SHIP tosses at anchor amidst savage waves.

33 INT. THE SHIP - THE 'TWEEN DECKS. NIGHT.   33

    The 'tween decks: near DARKNESS. A single flickering lantern
    swings wildly from a hook in the roof. Dripping water.
    Creaking walls as the ship LURCHES violently from side to
    side.

    The space heaves with terrified EMIGRANTS. WATER sprays
    through wrenched joints. The bilges are ankle-deep. PEOPLE
    groan and shout with panic in the dark. Children wail. Above
    all comes the regular, massive BOOM of heavy blows.

    In a bunk by the ladder: YANKO lies prostrate. He is green
    with sickness. He lurches over the side of his bunk and
    clasps a hand over his mouth. He hears the clatter of a bolt
    above and looks up over his shoulder, sees:

    THE HATCH atop the ladder opens for a moment and A STEWARD
    peers down. A SHOUT: the steward looks away, shouts back. The
    HATCH falls down.

    YANKO's EYES: narrow as he tries to focus on --

    THE HATCH: a chink of light shows it's not fully closed.

    YANKO clambers from his bunk, catches his balance, clutches
    his belly. He climbs the ladder -- opens the hatch --

    BELOW: The single swinging lamp shatters as a violent gust
    dashes it into the timbers. TOTAL DARKNESS FALLS. The panic
    and fear become more frantic -- more intense.

34 INT. THE SHIP - A NARROW GANGWAY. NIGHT.   34

    YANKO'S FACE appears in a yellow shaft of light as he rises
    from the hatch. He drags himself through and crawls out and
    down the gangway towards --

    A lamp bolted to the wall by a steep, wet wooden STAIR.

35 EXT. THE DECK. NIGHT.   35

    YANKO reels out of a hatchway and falls to his face.

                                        (CONTINUED)

35   CONTINUED: 35

      THE DECK stretches endlessly away before his eyes, lashed
      with rain and wind, rolling and pitching vertiginously.

      He scrambles to his knees. He throws up. Relieved, he manages
      to find his feet; loses his balance; reels across the rain-
      slicked planks, slips --

      He crashes into a STACK of large HENCOOPS lashed to the
      superstructure. He grips the wooden bars. Inside a dozen
      DUCKS squawk frantically in his face. He looks, sees:

      Tangled rigging. The gunwales. Beyond: utter darkness.

      YANKO blinks in the furious rain and noise of the gale - he
      has no idea where he is. A burst of frantic YELLING.

      A SEAMAN runs forward, desperately brandishing a LANTERN high
      in the air waving urgently to YANKO.

      Yanko takes a step back, frightened and confused, still   *
      holding onto the coop. A great wave looms high above him -   *
      almost hovers, a towering wall of water - and then falls,   *
      roaring and crashing towards him.   *

      YANKO is torn away and smashed to the deck. His hands still   *
      clutch the bars of the hencop - ripped from its lashings.   *
      The ducks squawk in his face. The deck tilts beneath him -   *

      Yanko and the coop start to slide.   *

      Another huge WAVE towers -- falls -- SWEEPS Yanko overboard.   *

36   EXT. NEW BARNS FARM.   36

      Apart from the rage of wind and rain the yard is quiet -- no
      sign of animals or men. The house stands in darkness.

37   EXT. THE BEACH. NIGHT.   37

      Darkness. Noise: the raging pandemonium of the sea.

      A shattered coop, full of drowned ducks. Nearby: YANKO lies
      unconscious on the shingle, wrapped in clinging strands of
      seaweed.

      38 - OMITTED

      39 - OMITTED

      40 - OMITTED

      41 - OMITTED

      42 - OMITTED

      43 - OMITTED

44- OMITTED   *

45 - OMITTED   *

46 - OMITTED

47 - OMITTED

48 - OMITTED   *

49   EXT. THE MOORS. DAY.   49

An open expanse of misty winter moorland rolls away into the
distance. In that distance: a lone, ragged figure - walking.

The fields rise gradually towards a ridge. Laboured panting
sounds. RISING up the hill -- above and beyond the ridge --

YANKO SEES -- in the middle distance -- NEW BARNS FARM.

50   INT. NEW BARNS FARM - THE KITCHEN. DAY.   50

MRS. SMITH approaches AMY - washing up at the sink - with a
dirty serving dish. Mrs. Smith freezes and SCREAMS with
terror. The dish drops and shatters on the stone flags.

AMY spins on Mrs. Smith -- then, following the terrified
gaze, Amy turns back to the window, SEES:

A FACE: barely recognizable as human - the features caked
with dirt and blood; long hair matted into tangled, dangling
locks. Wild EYES flit through the panes.

BEDLAM: Mrs. Smith shrieks in hysteria; the DOG snarls.

AMY is rapt. She is looking straight through the filthy,
bloody, exterior of the wild face outside into --

Yanko's eyes. Yanko's eyes stop flitting and find a sudden -
entranced - focus in --

AMY - a woman as calm and wonderful as an angel - and who
seems to look at - and see - him.

Yanko raises a hand tries to rub the dirt off his cheek.

Amy turns to see --

MRS. SMITH frantically throws the bolts on the kitchen door
as the snarling DOG scrabbles to get out.

                    AMY
          He means no harm.

Mrs. Smith looks at her as if she's lost her mind. She grabs
the dog's collar, drags it with her to the stairs.

                                              (CONTINUED)

19.

50   CONTINUED: 50

                              MRS. SMITH
                    Stay away from that window, you idiot
                    girl! And open the door to no one. NO
                    ONE!

          Mrs. Smith disappears. AMY turns back to the window.

          The WILD FACE has gone.

          Amy looks over at the door. She walks towards it.

51   EXT. NEW BARNS FARMYARD. DAY.   51

          MR. SMITH rides into the farmyard. He stops: from the house
          he hears the dog barking furiously.

                              MR. SMITH
                    Margaret? MARGARET!

52   INT. NEW BARNS FARM - THE KITCHEN. DAY.   52

          Amy's hands throw the bolts. She reaches for the handle as if
          to go outside -- steps back as --

          MR. SMITH pushes the door open, red faced.

                              SMITH
                    Amy? Why was the door locked? What's up
                    with that dog?

          Amy looks at him without answering. Smith - exasperated.

                              SMITH
                    Hell's bells, girl, what in damnation is
                    going on?

          Amy won't reply.

          Mrs. Smith - red eyed - sweeps into the room. She collapses,
          weeping, into Smith's arms.

                              MRS. SMITH
                    Oh Will! Thank God you're home!

          As the dog makes a snarling dash for the yard -- Amy darts
          forward and slams the door.

          MR. SMITH, bewildered, looks over his wife's sobbing shoulder
          at AMY. Amy stares back at him.

                              AMY
                    He means no harm.

53   EXT. THE FARMYARD - THE STACKS. DAY.   53

          A hidden POV: watching the house from amongst the stacks.
          From inside the house come muffled shouts.

54   INT. NEW BARNS - THE KITCHEN. DAY.   54

       SMITH, furious, grabs a gnarled stick from the stand.

                       SMITH
              There was talk about him in the village.
              He likes to frighten women and children
              this one! That's how they are, these
              lunatics.

                       AMY
              He means no harm.

                     MRS. SMITH
              What would you know of lunatics, you
              stupid girl? If you can't say anything
              sensible, be quiet!

       Smith stomps towards the door shaking his cudgel.

                     SMITH
              By Christ I'll teach the blackguard what
              it means to be 'frightened'.

       As Smith grabs the door handle, AMY rushes over and grabs the
       snarling dog by its collar, holds it back.

       SMITH wrenches the door open and storms outside.

55   EXT. THE FARMYARD. DAY.   55

       SMITH prowls about with his stick.

       AMY, crouches in the doorway, holds the dog, watches as-

       SMITH disappears into the STACKYARD.

56   EXT. THE STACKYARD. DAY.   56

       SMITH, belligerent, searches amongst the stacks. Suddenly he
       freezes: his belligerence pales into SHOCK.

       Sitting cross-legged amongst a pile of loose straw, swinging
       himself to and fro like a bear in a cage, is YANKO. He is
       barely recognizable as a human. He stops swinging and peers
       through the matted curtain of hair across his face.

       SMITH swallows and tightens his grip on his cudgel.

       Yanko stands UP. He raises his hands to part the matted hair:
       desperate eyes stare from a gashed, engrimed face.

       SMITH takes several steps backwards in fear.

       Bowing from the waist, Yanko stumbles forward. SMITH
       retreats, one step at a time, into the main yard.

57   EXT. THE FARMYARD. DAY.   57

        AMY watches SMITH back out from the stackyard. YANKO appears.
        AMY clasps her arms around the growling dog.

        MR. SMITH, gathering his wits, speaks firmly but gently as he
        backs away, Yanko still advancing.

                        SMITH
                Alright, my friend. Bear with me, now,
                and we'll see if between the two of us
                you and I can't sort something out...

        At the sound of the first remotely friendly voice he's heard,
        Yanko explodes into a stream of dialect:

                        YANKO
                Dyakuyu vam, pane, shcho dozvolily menee
                veedpochity na vasheey zemlee. Probachte,
                koly ya zavdav vam klopotu. Prisyahayu
                eemenem Boha, shcho ya dobriy cholovik,
                yak ee vy, povazhniy pane, dobriy
                cholovik...

        SMITH, smiling and nodding, glances over his shoulder as they
        enter the main yard. He sees --

        AMY crouched in the doorway; then he spots --

        THE WOOD LODGE.

        Smith backs towards it as YANKO continues --

                        YANKO
                Ya ne zhebrak, yakim vidayusya, ale
                beedniy podorozhneey, shcho yogo
                speetkalo likho --

        Suddenly SMITH CHARGES at him and PINS him against the wall
        of the wood lodge with his stick. Yanko struggles; but Smith
        is burlier and stronger.

                        SMITH
                Now we'll have you, you filthy
                blackguard.

        In the doorway: The dog springs loose from Amy's grip and   *
        streeks across the yard snarling. Amy sprints after it.   *

                        AMY   *
                Don't! Stop it!   *

        The dog snaps savagely at Yanko's legs, tearing further his   *
        already ragged garb. Yanko feels like he's fighting for his   *
        life. He looks at: Smith's panting face, inches from his own.   *
        He sees: the deep, uncomprehending fear in Smith's eyes.   *

(CONTINUED)

57   CONTINUED: 57

AMY grabs the dog and drags him away. Yanko - surprised -   *
looks as: the DOG, crazy, squirms, turns on AMY, snaps.   *

AMY jerks one hand away as the dog draws blood from her arm.   *

The sight gives Yanko a great surge of strength. With a   *
grunting shout he hurls Smith staggering backwards to fall on   *
the cobbles. Yanko rushes forward, grabs the dog by one ear   *
and its collar, twists it away from Amy. She lets go. The dog   *
scrabbling and squirming. For a second: *

Yanko's eyes meet Amy's. Then: *

THUD: Smith's cudgel smashes Yanko across the back of the   *
skull. Yanko falls unconsious, releasing the yelping dog.   *

                    SMITH   *
          Sammy! Down Boy! Down!   *

The dog backs off. Smith - trembling - looks at Yanko.   *

                    SMITH   *
          Christ Almighty!   *

He looks at Amy - who is staring at him furiously.   *

                    AMY   *
          He meant no harm!   *

Smith gapes, astonished, as Amy crouches down by Yanko.   *

                    SMITH   *
               (now angry)   *
          Get back inside, young lady. This minute.   *

Smith grabs Yanko by the ankles and drags him to the wood   *
lodge door. He sees Amy glaring at him.   *

                    SMITH   *
          This minute, I say! Go on!   *

ANGLE: through the wood lodge door -- Yanko lies unconsious   *
amidst wood chips and debris. The door slams shut.   *

58   INT. THE KITCHEN. DAY.   58

SMITH, relieved, puts his stick away, then LOOKS from --

AMY at the open door, looking out across the yard --

To -- MRS. SMITH -- trembling and prostrate in a chair.

Smith, exasperated, stomps to the stove and grabs the kettle.

(CONTINUED)

58   CONTINUED: 58

                         SMITH
              A dangerous lunatic - by all accounts an
              escaped maniac, no less - neatly dealt
              with for the protection of all. And not
              even so much as the offer of a decent cup
              of tea.

       59 - OMITTED   *

       60 - OMITTED   *

61   INT. THE KITCHEN. NIGHT.   61

       AMY walks silently across the kitchen in the moonlight. She
       opens the pantry door and goes inside.

62   EXT. NEW BARNS FARM. NIGHT.   62

       Mist clings to the cobbles. The back door opens.   *

       At the door: AMY'S FACE.   *

63   EXT/INT. THE WOOD LODGE. NIGHT.   63

       AMY slides the bolt. She opens the lodge door, sees:

       YANKO curled on the floor amongst dirt, wood chips, rubbish.
       He shivers and mumbles in his sleep.

       AMY stands looking at him for a long beat.

       Under her arm she carries a bundled blanket. She sets the   *
       bundle down. She crouches down and studies.   *

       His sleeping face - the matted hair and beard, the scar   *
       gashed across his cheekbone.   *

       Amy turns to unwrap the bundle; stops -- turns --   *

       YANKO'S EYES are wide open, staring at her.   *

       AMY holds his gaze.   *

       In the eerie sounds of the dawn, neither of them speak.   *

       YANKO rises slowly to his knees. His eyes widen as: *

       Amy reaches outside and pulls in the bowl of water. She wets   *
       and soaps a cloth - and raises it.   *

       He looks into her eyes - he's astonished; but entranced.   *

       Amy WASHES Yanko's face.   *

       AMY'S FACE: Watching, as --   *

                                                       (CONTINUED)

63   CONTINUED: 63

YANKO'S FACE emerges from beneath the grime.   *

Neither of them speaks.   *

Amy rinses the cloth. She washes his hands.   *

Yanko closes his eyes. His face trembles. He is immeasurably   *
moved - as he feels his humanity re-emerge from beneath the   *
filth. He opens his eyes as Amy hands him a towel.   *

YANKO HANDS - cut, bruised, but clean - hold the towel to his   *
face. He lowers the towel. He is transformed, not only   *
outwardly, but inwardly too.   *

AMY looks at him. Something has changed inside her too.   *

Yanko waits - uncertainly.   *

From the bundle she unwraps the paper from -- half a loaf of   *
BREAD. She holds it towards him.   *

                    AMY   *
          Can you eat this?   *

YANKO stares at the loaf. AMY holds it out closer. Yanko   *
takes the bread, as if it were a sacred object. His eyes   *
fill.   *

Amy watches him.   *

Suddenly Yanko falls to his knees and starts to devour the   *
bread. TEARS tumble down his face and fall upon the crust. He   *
is so moved he can barely swallow - barely breathe. He stops.   *
A convulsive sob wracks his body. Yanko drops the bread and   *
grabs hold of her wrist.   *

                    YANKO   *
          Laskava pannee...Laskava pannee.   *

He plants a KISS on her hand.   *

AMY: watches him.   *

Reverently, YANKO lets go of her hand. He clasps the bread to   *
his chest. Amy takes the blanket and stands up. She drapes   *
the blanket around his shouders, wraps it round him.   *

                    AMY   *
          Sleep.   *

She puts her head to her clapped hands. Yanko understands. He   *
lies down, huddled, looking at her in wonder as --   *

Amy backs out of the wood lodge and closes the door.   *

64   EXT. COLEBROOK BAY - THE SHINGLE BEACH. DAWN   64

The town. Beneath the sea wall a great sweep of BEACH. A
sullen dawn sky. The choppy grey immensity of the sea.

65   EXT. THE SEA - UNDERWATER. DAWN.   65

We drift through grey - almost black - water.

From the depths emerges an obscure shape -- a hulk -- a great
SHIP perched precariously on a shelf of rock.

Closer: in the ship's side is a huge, gaping HOLE.

The ship creaks and shifts in a current, teetering on the
edge of the shelf as it -- SLIPS over and starts to FALL.

From the hole emerges A TINY BODY. Around its neck glitters a
SILVER CRUCIFIX.

The little girl FLOATS up -- up towards the grey light.

66 - OMITTED   *

67 - OMITTED   *

67A   EXT. NEW BARNS FARM - THE YARD. DAWN.   67A

Amy walks back to the house through the dawn mist.

                    KENNEDY (V.O.)
              Such was the spark of compassion that
              ignited the fire of tragedy.

68   INT. MISS SWAFFER'S ROOM. NIGHT.   68

Kennedy straightens - satisfied - from the debrided leg.

The ULCER -- still raw, but now a clean, healthy red. The
yellow suppuration and gangrenous flesh has been excised.

                    MISS SWAFFER
              Tragedy, Doctor?

KENNEDY drops his instruments into a steel bowl, turns.

                    MISS SWAFFER
              The tragedy - if tragedy you must make it
              - began for Amy long before that night.
              The Foster's put Amy out to service at
              the earliest possible moment - the
              morning of her thirteenth birthday.

                    KENNEDY
              Is that so unusual?

                                        (CONTINUED)

68   CONTINUED: 68

                         MISS SWAFFER
                You know Isaac Foster only as a poor
                sheep herder - and Amy's mother as the
                harrowed and embittered woman you see
                today - but long before you came to these
                parts, Isaac was heir to a prosperous tin
                mine, by Truro.

Kennedy looks up questioningly.

                         MISS SWAFFER
                Isaac's father was a widower, engaged to
                be married to his cook, Mary. She ran
                away with Isaac - and five months later
                gave birth - to Amy. Isaac was disowned
                as punishment for the scandalous - and
                the Fosters have held Amy the cause of
                all their woes ever since.

                         KENNEDY
                No doubt it kept the town gossips happy
                for a year or two.

Miss Swaffer smiles, wanly, and nods. Then, with sorrow:

                         MISS SWAFFER
                No one can be crueller than those to whom
                one is closest. And the villagers forge
                gossip out of suffering to protect
                themselves - 'There but for the grace of
                God - go we all.'

At this Kennedy too becomes thoughtful - and sombre.

Quietly - a church bell starts to toll.

                         KENNEDY
                Quite so. Quite so...

69   EXT. COLEBROOK BAY. DAY.   69

      The water's edge. A tiny fair-haired child floats face-down
      in the shallows. The crucifix glitters dimly below the water.

      The bell - now louder, more frantic.

70   EXT. COLEBROOK HIGH STREET. DAY.   70

      The tolling echoes throughout the town as -- men and women -   *
      fear etched deep into every face - hurry down the cobbled   *
      main street. A man in a grimey apron emerges from the fish-   *
      smoker's shop - THACKERY. He sees PREBLE - the lame   *
      wheelwright - hobble past, and grabs his arm.   *

                                                      (CONTINUED)

70   CONTINUED: 70

                         THACKERY
          What's up?

                         PREBLE
          Ship down! In the bay!

     Preble pulls loose and hurries on. Thackery pulls off his
     apron, throws it into his shop and shuts the door. He runs
     down the street with the rest.

71   EXT. THE BEACH. DAY.   71

     The grey, surf-flecked sea. The bell tolling in the distance.
     Then --

     Along THREE MILES of shingle beach DARK FIGURES with bare
     legs dash in and out of the tumbling foam - dragging with
     them dark, limp, heavy shapes.

     CLOSER IN-SHORE:

     A long, irregular procession of townsfolk in PAIRS - men and
     women of all ages - crunch across the shingle towards the
     VILLAGE and its tolling spire.

     Each pair carries between them - on stretchers, on wattles,
     on ladders - a stiff, dripping corpse:

     Dead men, dead women, dead children.

     The faces of the villagers are drawn - haunted by the spectre
     that shadows all their lives: the sea. As each pair reaches
     the top of the beach they pause before --

     DOCTOR KENNEDY.

     KENNEDY'S FACE: as he looks down into the vacant eyes of:

     Yet another dead body: it is STEFAN. His face is pallid and
     slack. Kennedy feels for the neck pulse. At that moment the
     bell stops tolling. He closes Stefan's eyes.

     Kennedy shakes his head, appalled. He motions the stretcher
     bearers on. He pauses. He glances out at:

     THE GREY SEA: immense, inscrutable, pitiless.

                         WOMAN'S VOICE
          My boys! My boys! Please God not again!
          Where are my fine boys?

     An old woman - WIDOW CREE - her weathered face frantic with
     fear - comes stumbling down the the beach steps.

     The beach: the stretcher bearers stop in their tracks.

                                               (CONTINUED)

71 CONTINUED: 71

Widow Cree's eyes peer myopically - desperately - at the
bodies. KENNEDY takes her gently by the shoulders.

                    KENNEDY
            Don't fret for your boys, mother. It was
            an emigrant ship, bound for America. It
            wasn't one of our own.

                    WIDOW CREE
            Not one of our own?

As this sinks in a great - and terrible - relief swamps her
features. She clasps her hands and shouts to heaven:

                    WIDOW CREE
            Praises be! Praises be to God!

Her voice rolls out across the long - motionless and watching
- procession of death. As her voice fades it is answered by
the pounding of the surf.

Kennedy is shocked. He says nothing - but Mother Cree sees
his expression -- and realizes what she has said. The joy on
her face turns to horror. She claps her fists to her mouth.
She looks down at:

STEFAN - dead on the wattle.

                    WIDOW CREE
            The sea will curse me for those words. It
            is the Day of Judgement!

Her eyes roll with terror.

                    WIDOW CREE
            God forgive me! God forgive me!

She collapses into racking sobs. Kennedy holds her up. He
looks as all about him he hears the sound of --

Other women starting to cry with an eerie keening moan. In
the faces of the men too is a sudden - pagan - fear.

Kennedy senses mass hysteria. He raises his steady voice.

                    KENNEDY
            Quiet! Shhh! No one else is going to be
            cursed! No one amongst you! But we will
            see our duty done by this tragic day!

The keening dies down - but Widow Cree keeps on sobbing.
Kennedy motions two other women to take her.

                    KENNEDY
            Ladies, see that mother is cared for.

(CONTINUED)

71 CONTINUED: 71

        The ladies take the sobbing widow away. Kennedy turns to the
        still motionless procession on the beach.

                        KENNEDY
                Come along now! The rest of us have work
                to do!

        KENNEDY beckons a waiting pair of stretcher bearers.

                        KENNEDY
                Next.

        As the stretcher is borne to him - the widows sobs into the
        distance - the whole beach starts into motion again.

        72 - OMITTED

73 EXT. ST CHRISTOPHER'S CHURCH - COLEBROOK. LATER.   73

        A mass of townsfolk are gathered around at a respectful
        distance from the church. The rough-faced men are grimly
        silent. The women wear their everyday clothes, splashed here
        and there with bright colours - a red skirt, a white blouse,
        a blue shawl - yet each of them wears something BLACK on her
        head. A scarf, a hat, a scrap of linen. Many of the women   *
        weep; some clutch rosaries and murmur Hail Mary's.   *

        KENNEDY strides past them, CANON VAN STONE at his heels.
                                         AMENDED 3/9/96   *
                        VAN STONE   *
                The coast guard believes the emigrant   *
                ship was holed on the rocks off Pentire   *
                Head during the great storm on Sunday   *
                night. The shift of the morning tide must   *
                have disturbed the wreck.   *

        As they round the corner KENNEDY stops in his tracks.The
        colour drains from his face:

        Rolling outwards from his feet - in row upon grim row -
        HUNDREDS OF DEAD are laid out under the north wall of the
        church. Men -- women -- children --.

        KENNEDY pales - stunned by the scale of the horror.

                        Mrs.Rigby(O.S)
                Were you able to save any, Doctor?

        KENNEDY, is almost overcome. He collects himself; takes a
        deep breath; turns back to hold the Canon's vapid gaze.

                        KENNEDY
                I have looked into their each and every
                face. And there is not a solitary living
                soul amongst them.

                                                        (CONTINUED)

73   CONTINUED: 73

      Van Stone sees in Kennedy's face how deeply he has been
      affected by such intense proximity to the horror - he gropes   *
      for a response.

                              VAN STONE
                    'For the thing which I greatly feared is
                    come upon me, and that which I was afraid
                    of is come unto me -- '

      Kennedy turning back to the dead, interrupts, continues -

                              KENNEDY
                    'I was not in safety, neither had I rest,
                    neither was I quiet. Yet trouble came.'

      Kennedy is close to losing his composure. He regains it with
      brusque terseness. He looks at Van Stone.

                              KENNEDY
                    I am familiar with the Book of Job. These   *
                    souls are in your hands now - and the
                    ailments of the living do not wait upon
                    the dead.

      Kennedy wheels and strides away.

      The TOWNSFOLK watch him walk towards his Phaeton.

      KENNEDY, aware of their eyes upon him, carries himself with
      the strength he knows they need from him.

      Kennedy mounts the Phaeton and drives away.

74   EXT. NEW BARNS - THE FARMYARD. DAY.   74

      OLD SWAFFER walks with SMITH across the yard towards the wood
      lodge. SMITH is clearly somewhat in awe of him.

                              SMITH
                    Thank you for coming over so prompt, Mr.
                    Swaffer sir. I tell you, this character
                    we have here is madder than a March hare.

                              SWAFFER
                    Haven't seen a March hare in a good many
                    years. The last time I did, he seemed
                    much the same to me as any other variety.

                              SMITH
                    Perhaps you mistake my meaning, sir. It's
                    my belief - but not mine alone, of course
                    - that this creature has broken loose
                    from some kind of lunatic asylum. God
                    knows where. Your advice would be a
                    genuine comfort.
                        (Smith reaches for the door.)
                    Mind now! These maniacs do not lack for
                    cunning.

                                                      (CONTINUED)

Smith grips his stick, unbolts the door and cautiously eases
it open. His jaw drops.

YANKO, ragged but CLEAN - transformed - looks up at them.
Unsteadily - he stands up.

                         SMITH
            Watch yourself, sir! He's a fierce devil!

Swaying with fatigue, Yanko looks at Swaffer - pulls back his
shoulders with some semblance of dignity - of pride.

Swaffer - tugging his lip - studies him, silently intrigued.

Smith stares, shocked, at Yanko's improved condition.

                         SMITH
            Sir, I swear, when I wrestled him in here
            - and quite a scrap it was, too - he
            looked like the beast of Malkin Moor.
            Indeed, it crossed my mind that this was
            the very same --

He spots: the BLANKET round Yanko's shoulders.

Smith turns: AMY is standing behind them, watching.

                         SMITH
            You opened this door?

Amy stares at him. Smith glances back at Yanko.

                         SMITH
            Why you might have got us all murdered in
            our beds!

                         AMY
            He was dirty.

Smith is appalled. He looks at Amy as if she is a harlot.

                         SMITH
            You mean you washed him?
                (her eyes answer him)
            Good Christ. If you weren't such a
            helpless idiot I'd suspect unnatural
            practices.

Swaffer, still tugging his lip, hasn't taken his eyes off
Yanko and his long, tangled hair. Smith turns to Amy.

                         SMITH
            Get back to the house, young lady. Right
            now!

Amy and Smith stare at each other - Smith as if he barely
knows her. As he's about to raise his voice again --

                                                        (CONTINUED)

74   CONTINUED: 74

        Swaffer releases his lip.

                        SWAFFER
                I would suggest that this man would
                benefit - benefit highly, indeed - from
                the services of a good gentleman's
                barber.

        SMITH coughs and shuffles.

                        SWAFFER
                But as we both know - to our own cost -
                such is not available in these parts.

                        SMITH
                All too true, sir, all too true. You'll
                understand, then, if I say that I'm
                damned if I know what to do with him.

        Swaffer looks at Yanko and raises one eyebrow.

                        SWAFFER
                He is a funniosity.

        YANKO is looking into AMY's eyes.

75   EXT. NEW BARNS FARM - KITCHEN DOORWAY - FARMYARD. DAY.   75

        By the doorway AMY watches with unfathomable eyes as --

        A high two wheeled cart drawn by a white mare rattles across
        the yard. Swaffer holds the reins. Next to him is YANKO. He
        turns in his seat and looks back as --

        AMY - watches him go.

        YANKO calls out hoarsely.

                        YANKO
                Ya ne zabudu, laskava panee! Ne zabudu!
                Neekoly! Neekoly! Neekoly!

        AMY -- as Yanko's voice fades into the distance.

        SMITH glances at her as he walks past into the house.

                        SMITH
                Well, that's the last we'll see of him.

        Yanko raises his hand as the cart disappears, leaving --

        AMY: standing alone in the wintery yard.   *

        76 - OMITTED   *

        77 - OMITTED   *

77A   EXT. NEW BARNS FARM - THE YARD. SPRING.   77A*

The yard is transformed by spring - sunshine; blue sky; the   *
trees in leaf; birdsong; flowers blooming the window boxes.   *

Kennedy's carriage stands in the yard.   *

78   INT. NEW BARNS FARM - THE KITCHEN. DAY.   78

A rough HAND: a nasty gash in the palm is held together by
catgut stitches. Other hands cover it with lint guaze.

> KENNEDY
> The tendons are not severed. You were
> lucky.

SMITH, stoical, sits at the table as his cut is bandaged.

> SMITH
> It's lucky Malcolm caught you on the
> road.

> KENNEDY
> I am on my way to Swaffer's for our game
> of chess. We haven't played since the New
> Year and I have yet to get the better of
> him - but this new spring brings me hope.

> SMITH
> (lowers his voice)
> It is true, Doctor, that Old Swaffer will
> stay up 'til eleven o'clock of a night-
> time reading books?

> KENNEDY
> (amused)
> I have been known to stay up until ten
> myself.

> SMITH
> They also say he can write a cheque for
> two hundred pound without blinking an
> eye!

As they speak AMY comes up with a steaming kettle and
gestures to Kennedy's bowl, offering fresh water.

> KENNEDY
> I'm finished here, thank you. Amy, isn't
> it?

Amy nods without speaking.

> SMITH
> You'd better go now, Amy, or you'll catch
> it. Your father'll be expecting his
> Sunday lunch.

(CONTINUED)

78 CONTINUED: 78

    Amy curtsies. Smith watches walk away.

> SMITH
> I've a soft spot for her so I don't say
> this unkindly but she'll go from one week
> to the next without saying a word - and I
> swear to God she does not know how to
> smile.   *

  Amy taks her hat from a clothes peg in the hall and puts it on in   *
front of the mirror. She overhears SMITH in the kitchen.   *

> SMITH (O.S.)   *
> I reckon Isaac still blames her for   *
> losing his father's fortune. People   *
> aren't always fair, are they Doctor?   *
>   Revised 29/10/96

    Amy - still looking at herself in the mirror.   *

                                  CUT TO

79 EXT. THE BEACH. DAY.   79

    Light waves tumble up the beach. AMY - dressed in her Sunday
best - stands in the water, her face turned up to the breeze
and the sky. She holds her boots to her breast. Now alone,
her face shows something of the primal joy that she felt in
the storm. She starts to dance through the waves - whirling,
skipping. She stops as: a glint of light catches her eye.

    Washed up amongst some rocks on the sand is a string of three
glass fishing floats torn loose from a net. Amy picks them up
- pleased - and holds them up to the light.

    Colours refract through the glass.

    80 - OMITTED (NOW SCENE 85A)   *

81 INT. THE FOSTER'S COTTAGE. DAY.   81*

    AMY enters. The home of a poorly paid sheep herder.   *

    ISAAC FOSTER - surly - and three children between the ages of   *
nine and twelve sit sit eating at a scarred table.   *

    Foster's wife, MARY - a raw bitter woman worn down and out   *
beyond her forty years - turns from the wood stove.   *

> MARY   *
> You're late.   *

    Amy doesn't respond. She goes over and starts helping her   *
mother.   *

    Isaac sourly observes Amy's wet dress.   *

                                   (CONTINUED)

81 CONTINUED: 81

                         FOSTER   *
              Dillying and dallying on the beach, no   *
              doubt. I don't know why we still have her   *
              over.   *

                         MARY   *
              She comes to help her mother, not for   *
              your benifit.   *

                         FOSTER   *
              She's a queer sort. Always has been.   *
                                     Revised 29/10/96

                         MARY
              Is it any wonder? The way you treat her   *
              would silence the birds in the blessed   *
              trees.   *

AMY'S FACE - as she busies herself with the dishes - trying   *
to blot out the mounting - and familiar - conflict around   *
her.   *

                         FOSTER   *
              I put food in her mouth and a roof over   *
              her head.   *

                         MARY   *
              She puts food on our table now and don't   *
              you forget it.   *

Isaac scowls bitterly.   *

                         FOSTER   *
              I wish I could forget. She's a bloody   *
              embarrassment!   *

Amy: a flicker of pain.   *

                         MARY   *
              Isaac!   *

                         FOSTER   *
              Dancing in the rain like something not   *
              right. Picking up rubbish from the beach.   *

Amy turns away.   *

                         FOSTER   *
              They all know, tha knows. Jack Vincent   *
              swears the girl doesn't even know how to   *
              smile.   *

                         MARY   *
              If you spent less on grog you wouldn't   *
              care what that drunken swine thinks.   *

Foster looks at Mary with great bitterness.   *

                                              (CONTINUED)

81   CONTINUED: 81

                              FOSTER   *
                    If I spent less on grogg? How do you   *
                    think I tolerate this vale of bloody   *
                    tears?   *

Mary is stricken.   *

Amy wheels on Foster.   *

                                              Revised 29/10/96

                              AMY
                    Stop it! Do you hear me now? Stop it!   *

For a moment Foster is shocked into silence. Mary is also   *
amazed.   *

Foster rallies.   *

                              FOSTER   *
                    Well, what's gotten into you all of a   *
                    sudden, bright spark?   *

Amy kisses the children and picks up her hat.   *

                              FOSTER   *
                    Where do you think you're going?   *

Amy walks towards the door.   *

                              FOSTER   *
                    I'm talking to you, lady!   *

Amy slams the door behind her.   *

       82 - OMITTED

83   EXT. THE FOSTERS' COTTAGE. DAY.   83

       Amy walks away from the cottage. Whatever she feels about the
       strife she leaves behind, she does not show it.

84   EXT. THE FIELDS - THE DRY STONE WALL. DAY.   84

       AMY down the hill. She hears -- strange singing. From beyond
       the hedge.

       Amy walks towards the hedge. She looks - and listens --

       In the mid-distance the three NORWAY PINES tower from the
       rocky outcrop. Sitting against one of them is YANKO. His
       voice drifts across the escarpment.

       CLOSER: Yanko sits against the pines singing a majestic,
       melancholy song in his dialect. Beside him is a tin plate   *
       with the remains of his lunch - an apple core, a heel of   *
       bread.   *

                                                      (CONTINUED)

84   CONTINUED: 84

He suddenly stops singing and turns - aware. He sees:

Only: the hills, the patchwork of hedges and dry walls.

YANKO scratches his neck. He picks up his plate and starts   *
down the hill.   *

From her hidden spot AMY watches Yanko stride away.

                    AMY
          Come again, my beauty. Come again.

85 - OMITTED (NOW SCENE 85B)   *

85A   EXT. SWAFFER'S FARM - GARDEN. DAY.   85A*

The chessboard table in the sunlight. A bony hand moves a   *
black knight - placing the white king under seige.   *

                    SWAFFER   *
          Check.   *

KENNEDY frowns at Swaffer - who leans back inscrutably.   *

From the porch MISS SWAFFER - in black - watches them play   *
from her wheelchair.   *

Kennedy studies the board with some desperation.

                    KENNEDY   *
          I'll be damned, sir, if you don't have me   *
          again.   *

Kennedy looks up and SEES --   *

YANKO - wheeling a barrow full of earth at the foot of the   *
garden. Kennedy is intrigued.   *

                    KENNEDY   *
          I know you have a hard heart at chess,   *
          Swaffer, but don't your labourers get   *
          their half-a-day on the Sabbath?   *

Swaffer looks over at Yanko. He waves him over.   *

                    SWAFFER   *
          Don't know if that's rightly what you'd   *
          call him. Smith caught him in the   *
          stackyard at New Barns, reckons him to be   *
          a lunatic.   *

Kennedy stands as -- Yanko comes up. Their eyes meet.   *
Something passes between them. Yanko bows.   *

                                                          (CONTINUED)

85A   CONTINUED: 85A

                         SWAFFER   *
               Lunatic or not, he knows his way about a   *
               farm. You've been all over the world   *
               now, Doctor, so tell me. Don't you think   *
               this is a bit of a Hindoo we've got here?   *

YANKO gives up trying to follow the incomprehensible   *
exchange. Then - with sudden agitation - he sees --   *

The chess board. He turns -- then quietens as he finds: *

KENNEDY studying Yanko's olive complexion and bone structure,   *
his lithe build and shiney hair.   *

                         KENNEDY   *
               Unless he has undergone an unlikely   *
               conversion he is no Hindu. He puts me   *
               somewhat in mind of the Basque people.   *

SWAFFER raises an eyebrow. Kennedy, a little self-   *
consciously, coughs and turns to Yanko.   *

                         KENNEDY   *
               Hablar Espagnol, senor? Eres en   *
               Inglaterra. Inglaterra.   *

YANKO: uncomprehending. Kennedy tries again.   *

                         KENNEDY   *
               Parlez-vous Francais? Comprenez-vous?   *

No luck: KENNEDY signs; then reacts as --   *

                         YANKO
               Thank you, sir.   *

                         SWAFFER   *
               He's picked up a word or two from the   *
               daughter there. Seems to call himself   *
               'Yanko Goorall'.   *

Yanko nods and pokes himself in the chest.   *

                         YANKO   *
               Yanko.   *
                    (then eagerly)   *
               Please.   *

Kennedy indicates the board with his hand.   *

                         KENNEDY   *
               By all means.   *

Yanko bends over the board, his eyes flitting rapidly back   *
and forth. Kennedy and Swaffer wait in suspense.   *

Suddenly Yanko's hand darts out and advances a white pawn -   *

                                              (CONTINUED)

85A CONTINUED: 85A

taking the king out of check, threatening the knight, and   *
discovering a bishop attack on the black queen.   *

Even Swaffer looks astonished.   *

                    SWAFFER   *
          Well, he's got you out of trouble.   *

Kennedy - tremendously excited - turns to Yanko.   *

                    KENNEDY   *
          Moscow! Tolstoy! Chekov! Damn - think,   *
          man.   *

Kennedy sees Swaffer looking at him as if <u>he's</u> the lunatic.   *

                    KENNEDY   *
          The Volga! Kiev!   *

Yanko's face lights up with excitement.   *

                    YANKO   *
          Thank you! Thank you!   *
            (in Ukrainian)   *
          Kiev is the great city of my country,   *
          far from the mountains.   *

                    KENNEDY   *
          You see, Swaffer! A Russian!   *

                    SWAFFER   *
          A Russian?   *

                    KENNEDY   *
          Precisely! They are great players of   *
          chess, are they not?   *

                    YANKO   *
            (Ukrainian)   *
          I made a journey to America.   *

The word 'America' hits Kennedy like a thunderbolt. He turns   *
- sombre - to Swaffer.   *

                    KENNEDY   *
          How long has this man been here?   *

                    SWAFFER   *
          Since late winter - a couple of months.   *

                    KENNEDY   *
          When exactly?   *

                    SWAFFER   *
          The daughter's better with dates than I   *
          am.   *

                                              (CONTINUED)

85A CONTINUED: 85A

He turns to call MISS SWAFFER - but she is wheeling herself   *
forward.   *

                    MISS SWAFFER   *
          It was Febuary the eighteenth.   *

                    KENNEDY   *
          The eighteenth? You're quite sure?   *

Miss Swaffer nods. Kennedy - now moved - looks at Yanko.   *

                    KENNEDY   *
          The day that the sea gave up its dead.   *
          Swaffer -- you have here the only   *
          survivor from the Eastbay disaster - of   *
          appalling memory.   *

                    SWAFFER   *
          The shipwreck? But that part of the   *
          coast's a good twenty miles from Smiths   *
          farm.   *

                    KENNEDY   *
          Be that as it may, Febuary eighteenth is   *
          not a day that I will ever forget.   *

Kennedy steps towards Yanko and offers his hand.   *

                    KENNEDY   *
          Dr. James Kennedy.   *

Yanko hesitates, looks to Swaffer - who nods. Yanko takes   *
Kennedy's hand. Kennedy points a finger to his own chest.   *

                    KENNEDY   *
          Kennedy.   *

                    YANKO   *
          Kennedy.   *

Kennedy nods, pleased.   *

                    MISS SWAFFER   *
          Do you think he knows - that all his   *
          companions perished?   *

Kennedy looks at her; then at Yanko. Yanko's face is shining   *
with excitement - and hope.   *

                    KENNEDY   *
          I don't know.   *

                    MISS SWAFFER   *
          I think he has a right to know.   *

(CONTINUED)

41.

85A CONTINUED: 85A

                          KENNEDY   *
              No - I forbid it.   *
                (catches himself; more gently)   *
              To your great credit you have restored   *
              him to health. But the shock of such   *
              news - well, clinically speaking, I   *
              couldn't be responsible for the effect it   *
              might have on his mind. After all, we   *
              have no language by which to offer him   *
              comfort.   *

     Miss Swaffer - reluctantly - bows to Kennedy's authority.   *
     Kennedy - more brightly - turns to Swaffer.   *

                          KENNEDY   *
              If you could spare him from his work from   *
              time to time, it would please me to try   *
              to teach him English.   *

                          SWAFFER   *
              I don't see why not. Perhaps you could   *
              get him to teach you chess. Then your   *
              visits might be worth your making the   *
              journey.   *

     Swaffer - as always - remains deadpan.   *

     Kennedy bursts into laughter.   *

     And Yanko - for the first time since the ship - smiles.   *

85B INT. KENNEDYS HOUSE - THE STUDY. NIGHT.   85B*

     Yanko and Kennedy sit across a chess board. Kennedy picks up   *
     a rook to make A MOVE. YANKO SHAKES HIS HEAD.   *

                          YANKO   *
              No, Kennedy. Move - ah - no good.   *

                          KENNEDY
                (corrects him)
              That is not a good move

                          YANKO
              That is not a good move..... 'Precisely'

     Kennedy is amused - pleased - by his checkiness

                          KENNEDY
              You learn English faster than I learn
              chess.

                          YANKO   *
              The Miss help I - 'me'.   *

                                                    (CONTINUED)

42.

85B CONTINUED: 85B

>   KENNEDY
>   That's right. Miss Swaffer?

>   YANKO
>   (nods)
>   Why the Miss is in the cart- chair?

>   KENNEDY
>   Some twenty years ago, I am told, she was
>   engaged to be married. On the eve of the
>   wedding day she fell from her horse - it
>   seems she had a passion for riding - and
>   broke her spine.

Kennedy indicates a chopping gesture to his own back.

>   KENNEDY
>   It is a tribute to her spirit that she
>   has survived so long. The marriage was
>   quietly forgotten - by her intended, if
>   not by her.

>   YANKO
>   This why she wears always the clothes of
>   black?

>   KENNEDY
>   I had never thought of that, but it would
>   certainly be reason enough to do so.

>   YANKO
>   Why you are not have married, Kennedy?

>   KENNEDY
>   Oh, I was. A lifetime ago. Two lifetimes,
>   in fact - my wife and child. A son. The
>   typhus epidemic of '74 took them both on
>   the same night.

>   YANKO
>   But you do not wear the black.

>   KENNEDY
>   No.

KENNEDY looks over at: a framed portrait on the wall - A
formal seated pose: The YOUNG KENNEDY - sternly handsome -
with a STRIKING WOMAN. On her knee is a young boy in a little
suit.

Kennedy: difficult feelings; he suppresses them.

>   YANKO
>   Chess like the life, Yes? You must look
>   to the forward. Far to the forward.

(CONTINUED)

85B   CONTINUED: 85B

He makes a hopping gesture forwards with his hand - then   *
watches Kennedy's face as he makes a move.   *

                    YANKO   *
            Checkmate.   *

Kennedy looks at Yanko's - bashfull - smiling face - and   *
hasn't got the heart to talk again of death. Kennedy smiles -   *
this time with genuine warmth.   *

                    KENNEDY   *
            You are a cad, sir.   *

                    YANKO   *
                (proudly)   *
            I am a 'cad-sir'?   *

Kennedy laughs. He stands. They walk to the door.   *

                    KENNEDY   *
            Perhaps you would like to ride to Darford   *
            Market with me someday.   *

                    YANKO   *
            I can go only here with you, not other   *
            wheres.   *

                    KENNEDY   *
            That's bloody ridiculous. I will have   *
            words with Swaffer about that.   *

                    YANKO   *
            No! They are goodness. And I must make my   *
            own path to the forward. I must find my   *
            own gold.   *
                (smiles)   *
            Like a cad-sir.   *

85C   EXT. A COUNTRY ROAD. DAY.   85C*

MR. Swaffer drives a wagon. The rear of the wagon is loaded   *
with raw timber. Sat on the timber are Yanko and Issac   *
Foster.   *

Yanko looks at the landscape as if in recognition.   *

                    YANKO   *
            We go where, Foster?   *

                    FOSTER   *
            Smith's farm.   *

                    YANKO   *
            There is a girl, yes? At the farm.   *

(CONTINUED)

85C CONTINUED: 85C

                         FOSTER   *
               A girl? You don't mean our Amy?   *

                         YANKO   *
               Amy? Perhaps it is her name - yes? A   *
               gracious lady. A gracious lady of great   *
               beautiful.   *

Foster with bitter amusement.   *

                         FOSTER   *
               You'd have to travel a damm sight further   *
               than I ever have to find a gracious lady.   *
               As for 'great beautiful', the only girl   *
               I'm aware of at New Barns is my so-called   *
               daughter, Amy - and she's nobody's idea   *
               of an oil painting.   *

Yanko stricken with embarrassment.   *

                         YANKO   *
               Your daughter! Forgive me. I did not want   *
               to be not with respect.   *

Foster laughs callously.   *

                         FOSTER   *
               To our Amy you'd have as much chance with   *
               Swaffer's mare - and a better time of it   *
               too, I shouldn't wonder.   *

Yanko vaugely detects an insult - which amuses Foster the   *
more. He chuckles and slaps Yanko on the arm.   *

85D INT. NEW BARNS FARM - YARD DAY.   85D*

Amy reacts as she sees: *

Yanko and Foster on the wagon as it pulls into the yard.   *

Mrs. Smith - nervous - calls to Amy on her way to the door.   *

                         MRS. SMITH   *
               Amy? Put the kettle on, sharp now. And   *
               get the Royal Doulton cups out.   *

Mrs. Smith greets Swafffer as he gets down from the wagon.   *

                         MRS. SMITH   *
               Mr Swaffer, you've brought the lumber.   *
               William will be so pleased.   *

                         SWAFFER   *
               He hasn't heard the price yet.   *

                                            (CONTINUED)

45.

85D   CONTINUED: 85D

                              MRS. SMITH   *
                             (stiff smile)   *
                  Please, come in and have some tea.   *

         Foster jumps down from the wagon.   *

                              FOSTER   *
                  Cup of tea'd be right civilised, Mrs.   *
                  Smith.   *

         Mrs. Smith turns - shrinks back as -   *

         Yanko appears behind Foster   *

                              SWAFFER   *
                  You two wait out here   *

85E   EXT. NEW BARNS FARM. STONE WALL . DAY.   85E*

         Yanko and Foster sit on a low stone wall. Yanko - in an agony   *
         of shy excitment - stands up as he sees: *

         AMY emerge from the house carrying a tray. She stops for an   *
         instant as her eyes meet --   *

         Yanko - looking back across the yard, wringing his cap.   *
         Foster - still sitting - takes this in with a sly glee.   *

         Amy comes up to them, sets down the tray: two mugs of tea,   *
         two slices of fruitcake. Yanko bows.   *

                              YANKO   *
                  Thank you, Miss. Thank you.   *

                              FOSTER
                  Ah! Cake! We are honoured today.

         Amy curtsies, briefly, to Yanko. They're both acutely aware
         of Foster's presence. She turns to leave.

                              FOSTER
                             (eating)
                  Hold on, Amy, haven't you got a minute
                  for your poor old father?

         Amy hesitates - caught, embarassed. Yanko is confused by the
         strange dynamics. Amy nods to Foster.

                              AMY
                  Father.

                              FOSTER
                  This lad here thinks you're 'a gracious
                  lady' did you know that?

                                                        (CONTINUED)

46.

85E CONTINUED: 85E

Amy squirms inside. She can't look at Yanko.

>   FOSTER
>   'Of great beautiful' too, apparently.
>   Though now that I think about it, you do
>   look quite fetching in that pinny.

Amy wheels round and hurries away. Yanko - feeling her very
real distress - watches her go. Foster cackles then finds -
Yanko looking at him - angrily.

>   FOSTER
>   She can't take a joke, you see.
>   (taunting)
>   Well, let me give you a few tips on
>   courting. You take your money - you know
>   (he jingles some coins in his pocket)
>   - and you buy her some flowers. Or some
>   chocolates -
>   Oh, and you'll have to smarten yourself
>   up. Can't go courting looking like that -

Yanko either has to punch him or leave. He strides away
across the yard. Foster picks up the plate.

>   FOSTER
>   Don't you want your cake?   *

85F EXT. THE HILLS - SWAFFER'S FARM. DUSK.   85F

Yanko sits on the hill beneath his pine tres. In a dark mood,
he is whittling angrily on a piece of wood. Beside him lies a
plate of food - untouched.

85G EXT. THE CLIFFS ABOVE THE BEACH. DUSK.   85G*

AMY stands on the cliff top above the sound of the surf. She   *
too is troubled. In her hand she holds - the glass floats.   *
She raises them up to catch the golden, ferracted light of   *
the setting sun -- but it doesn't make her feel any better.   *

Crestfallen, the floats dangling by her side, she starts down   *
a rocky path to the beach and disappears.   *

86 - OMITTED   *

87   EXT. SWAFFER'S HOUSE - THE BACK GARDEN. DAY.   87

SWAFFER, MISS SWAFFER, WILLCOX and MRS. WILLCOX. They are   *
drinking tea and chatting.

From the back door totters a three year old GIRL in a white
pinafore. She toddles across the terraced garden towards:

A LOW WALL.

88   EXT. SWAFFERS FARM - THE FIELD. SUMMER DAY.   88*

Not far beyond the yard Yanko is digging a drainage ditch in
the blazing sun, laying six-inch clay pipes. He's sweating
and covered in mud. Sitting on a stack of pipes, smoking -
watching Yanko sweat is - Issac Foster. Yanko pauses to look
up at him.

                    FOSTER
          I'm paid to heard sheep not dig tunnels
          for someone else's shit. Swaffer's
          forgotted what century we're in.

As Yanko turns back, something catches his eye and - he drops
his tools and vaults from the ditch.

                    FOSTER
     Oi!

Yanko - hair flowing - sprints with long, atheletic strides
towards THE FARMHOUSE -

89   EXT. THE HOUSE - THE BACK GARDEN. DAY.   89

The low garden wall -- on the far side there is a five-foot
drop into a HORSE-POND. The toddler CHILD wallows helplessly
- face down in the muddy water.

THE HOUSE: MRS WILLCOX happens to glance out the window. She
does a double take - amazement; fear - as she sees:

The wild figure of YANKO bounding towards the house. He
disappears from view under the edge of the garden wall.

MRS. WILLCOX: rushes out the back door and pauses on the
threshold. Panic emerges on her face as her eyes search back
and forth across the empty yard.

                    MRS WILLCOX
          Bertha? BERTHA!

Mrs. Willcox is startled as:

YANKO springs up over the wall clutching: little BERTHA,
drenched in water and mud. He runs up the garden towards:

MRS WILLCOX: almost weeping with relief. She accepts THE
CHILD as Yanko - with his muddy hands - thrusts her into her
arms. Before she can speak her gratitude

YANKO turns and strides away.

Mrs. WILLCOX stares. MR WILLCOX joins her, fussing the child
in relief.

From within the doorway behind them SWAFFER'S FACE juts out
over their heads. His cool grey eyes narrow.

90   INT. SWAFFER'S DINING ROOM. EVENING.   90

The door opens and SWAFFER shows the hesitant YANKO inside.
It is clearly his first time indoors. He looks around the
room in awe, sees in the corner:

MISS SWAFFER sitting in her bathchair by the Welsh dresser.
Astonishingly, her thin lips curl into a mysteriously ironic
SMILE. She wheels over and motions him to come to --

The dinner table: set for one -- with fine cutlery and bone
china. Miss Swaffer indicates the chair. Yanko hesitates.

                    MISS SWAFFER
          Sit down!

Yanko sits. He barely dares touch the cutlery. Miss Swaffer
leans forward and takes the lid off a large plate of food.
She speaks as one might to the deaf.

                    MISS SWAFFER
          Eat!

YANKO crosses himself and picks up the knife and fork.

91   THE SAME - LATER.   91

Yanko, eating. Swaffer's gnarled hand appears and places by
the plate a small brown envelope. YANKO looks at it, puzzled,
then up at Swaffer. Swaffer nods.

                    SWAFFER
          It'll be regular from now on.

YANKO opens the envelope and tips into his palm TWO FLORINS.
He stares at the coins in his hand as if they are rare
jewels.

Speechless, Yanko looks up at Swaffer. Swaffer - as usual
giving no clues - strokes the back of a finger across his
hairy nostrils - and walks away.

Yanko - the coins in his open palm - looks at the Miss.

                    MISS SWAFFER
          It's money! From now on you'll work
          daylight hours with Sunday's off. And
          what you do in your own time's your own
          business. Now you finish your dinner!

Miss Swaffer turns her chair and creaks away to the door.

YANKO stares down at his coins.   *

                                                    (CONTINUED)

49.

92 - OMITTED   *

93   EXT. THE DARNFORD ROAD. DAY.   93*

      Kennedy's phaeton spins along the road; Yanko sits beside   *
      him.   *

      94 - OMITTED   *

95   EXT. DARNFORD. DAY.   95

      THE PHAETON comes hurtling down the road. YANKO is driving --
      singing a wild and stirring song.

      KENNEDY gamely clings on.

      DARNFORD: up ahead.

96   EXT. DARNFORD HIGH STREET. DAY.   96

      The phaeton moves along the street at a sedate pace. YANKO
      feels like a lord. Kennedy indicates to stop.

      Kennedy climbs down and mops his brow.

                        KENNEDY
                We'll take luncheon in The King's Head at
                one o'clock. Enjoy the market.

      YANKO watches him disappear.

97   EXT. DARNFORD MARKET. DAY.   97

      YANKO gapes in awe at the rich multiplicity of A BUSY MARKET.

      His eyes wide, flitting here - there - as something exotic
      catches his attention at every turn, Yanko wanders through
      the stalls. The merchandise is hugely more varied and opulent
      than anything he has ever seen. With his odd bearing he
      attracts many stares.

      Then Yanko SPOTS something. He strides over --

98   INT. THE KING'S HEAD. LUNCHTIME.   98

      KENNEDY: at a table, reading. He looks up as --

      YANKO enters. He's dressed in cheap but durable corduroys and
      a cambrick shirt. He puts two brown paper packages - one
      large, one small - on the table.

                        KENNEDY
                My, my. I thought for a moment it was the
                Prince of Wales.

      Yanko vaguely grasps the meaning of this, indicates his new
      clothes, shakes his head

                                                    (CONTINUED)

98   CONTINUED: 98

                         YANKO
              These strong, and well. But I have
              better.

YANKO carefully opens the large package and proudly reveals a
patch of rough, tweedy cloth.

                         YANKO
              A suit - real, like yours.

                         KENNEDY
              Very handsome, I'm sure. And the other?

Yanko picks up the small package. He hesitates, almost
blushes apologetically.

                         YANKO
              This is my mystery.

                         KENNEDY
              You mean your secret.

                         YANKO
              My secret. Yes.

                         KENNEDY
              Well, every man is entitled to his
              secrets, especially a man who owns a fine
              suit.

YANKO grins and puts the small package in his pocket. Then
more gravely, he produces an envelope and shows Kennedy.

                         YANKO
              This money, I want for to give my family.
              But I do not know the way.

Kennedy is touched.

                         KENNEDY
              We will go to the post office later.
                   (smiles)
              And now, I have an appetite.

He waves to the landlord. And Kennedy is glowing - he has
never looked better - so relaxed and content. He smiles.

                         KENNEDY
              You know, if I were my own physician I
              should instruct myself to do this more
              often.

99   INT. NEW BARNS FARM - THE KITCHEN. DAY.   99

AMY kneels scrubbing the stone flags. She does this - as all
her tasks - matter of factly and without a sense of being
hard-done by. Mrs. SMITH walks past on her way out of the
room as if Amy is invisible.

                                                    (CONTINUED)

99   CONTINUED: 99

There is a rapping on the back door. Amy gets to her feet,
dries her roughened hands on her dress. She opens the door.

YANKO stands on the threshold, squeezing his cap. He is
splendid - if self-conscious - in his new slop-made salt and
pepper suit. He looks at her as if the door has opened upon
an angel. He can't speak.

AMY'S FACE: her deep eyes silently drink him in.

YANKO, struggling for words, bows from the waist.

                    YANKO
              Gracious lady --

He falters. Amy just looks at him. Beneath her quiet surface
her heart is in her mouth.

                    YANKO
              Forgive me --

He suddenly fumbles in his pocket and produces the brown
paper package. He thrusts it out towards her.

                    YANKO
              Forgive me.

AMY looks at the package for what seems like ages. Then she
takes it.

Carefully, Amy starts to unwrap the package.

Yanko watches in an agony of excitement.

A GREEN SATIN RIBBON tumbles out into Amy's hands.

HER EYES: her heart is bursting. But she says nothing. She
wraps the ribbon back up with as much care as she opened it.

YANKO watches with baited breath.

AMY slips the ribbon in her APRON. She looks at him.

                    AMY
              Thank you.

YANKO beams - overcome with relief. His hands flutter.

                    YANKO
              Thank you - thank you. I would like --
              With your accepting -- If you would be
              pleased - forgive me - I should like -- I
              should like to walk out with you.

AMY: almost impassive - yet intensely moved. She gives a
barely perceptible NOD.

                                                    (CONTINUED)

99 CONTINUED: 99

                    YANKO
            You will? You will like to walk out with
            me?

AMY nods again, this time more clearly. YANKO melts. He bows
again. A few words of Ukranian escape him.

                    YANKO
            Nai presvyataya Diva blagoslovyt' tebe.

Yanko catches himself, continues in English.

                    YANKO
            Forgive me. Thank you. Blessings. When
            may I call again?

                    AMY
            On Sunday.

                    YANKO
            On Sunday? The next new Sunday?

AMY: another endless pause.

                    AMY
            Sunday is my day.

YANKO bows. Amy gives a curtsy -- and closes the door.

She turns back to the scrub bucket. She briefly touches the
pocket of her apron - and the work no longer seems arduous.
She kneels down and starts scrubbing furiously.

100 EXT. THE FIELDS. DAY. 100

ISAAC FOSTER sits on a hillock sullenly watching the sheep.
His head snaps up as he hears a WILD CRY.

On the ridge YANKO is leaping in the air, waving his cap,
shouting in his native tongue.

FOSTER'S reaction: a disgusted sneer as --

Yanko skims away across the grass.

101 EXT. NEW BARNS FARMYARD. DAY. 101

MR. SMITH being driven in a cart by his labourer, Malcolm. He
stops dead and his jaw drops as he sees:

YANKO - in a suit - knock on the back door.

                    SMITH
            What did I tell you? The man must be some
            kind of epileptic.

                                        (CONTINUED)

101 CONTINUED: 101

         Smith walks belligerently towards Yanko -- then stops in
         amazement for the second time as:

         The back door of the house opens and AMY FOSTER steps out in
         her FINERY: grey dress, hat, boots, white cotton gloves. At
         her throat is tied a GREEN SATIN BOW.

         Yanko offers her his arm. She takes it.

         Amy and Yanko walk out of the yard.

                         SMITH
                   Well I never did! I hope you know what
                   you're up to young lady!

         Smith is ignored. Then he sees MRS. SMITH returning from
         church in her landau. Mrs. Smith stares at Amy and Yanko in
         scandalized horror -- then turns on her husband.

                         MRS. SMITH
                   William? William! Why don't you do
                   something?

                         SMITH
                      (under his breath)
                   And there was me looking forward to a
                   nice quiet Sunday afternoon..

102 EXT. A SUNLIT WOOD. DAY.   102

         Oak and birch and yew. A mass of bluebells shift and swirl in
         a warm breeze. AMY strolls along in her finery, looking
         ahead, head high. Beside her, his coat slung over one
         shoulder, casting tender glances at her, walks YANKO.
                                                   AMENDED 3/9/96
         All around them is the glory of the summer.

103 EXT. THE MOORS. DAY.   103

         Amy and Yanko walk - still in silence - across rugged
         moorland towards a steep escarpment. They pause at the foot.
         Amy points up at the ridge. Beyond it: blue sky.

                         AMY
                   Is it too far?

                         YANKO
                   I am a highlander - a mountaineer!

         He grins and starts up the hill ahead of her.

104 EXT. THE HILL - THE RIDGE. DAY.   104

         Hand in hand, Amy and Yanko approach the ridge, the sky.
         Closer. They crest the ridge. And stop. Amy looks at:

                                                        (CONTINUED)

104   CONTINUED: 104

YANKO's FACE - he is stunned.

Below and beyond them, shimmering away in the heat haze to
the far blue horizon, spreads --

THE FRIGID SPLENDOUR OF THE SEA.

AMY glows at the rolling majesty of an old friend. She turns
to him proudly - stops:

YANKO is awe-struck but at the same time -- uneasy.

                    YANKO   *
          I - I never saw such a thing.   *

                    AMY   *
          Why, it's the sea. The ancient sea. The   *
          dark sea. The cruel sea. That's where you   *
          came from.   *

                    YANKO   *
          Yes. Yes - but it was then to me a black   *
          thing - howling, angry - like a monster.   *
                (his eyes: strangely haunted)   *
          This too is the sea.   *
                                           AMENDED 3/9/96
                    AMY   *
          It's where all the hearts of the earth -   *
          that have been lost to love and to fear -   *
          lie waiting to be reborn.   *

Yanko's breath is taken away.

                    YANKO
          That is not Christian.

He says it as if unsure if that is wonderful or terrible. He
looks at her -- and is swept away by the wonder. Entranced by
her face looking out to sea - he reaches out and strokes her
hair. He takes her chin and turns her towards him.

Amy glances at his lips. She closes her eyes; lifts her face
towards him. He hesitates, then -- kisses her on the mouth -
the merest touch.

Amy's eyelids flutter.

Yanko pulls back. They look at each other. Her eyes so swim
that Yanko is uncertain he has done the right thing.

Amy's eyes clear and focus. She looks at him.

AMY reaches up and takes his face in both hands -- and kisses
him with great passion.

Yanko throws his arms around her and pulls her to his chest.
Her arms encircle him. Yanko looks out at:

                                                      (CONTINUED)

104 CONTINUED: 104

The glittering blue of the sea.

Amy - her face against his chest - is crying silently.

105 - OMITTED

106 THE SAME - LATER.   106

Yanko and Amy stand on the ridge, a black, entwined
silhouette against the sky, as the light fades and the sun
goes down into the sea.

107 INT. NEW BARNS. THE KITCHEN. EVENING.   107

SMITH ploughs through his evening meal. MRS. SMITH,
ostentatiously picks without appetite. AMY waits on.

                    SMITH
                (chewing)
            You must be mad yourself, girl - to take
            up with a man who is surely wrong in the
            head.

AMY'S FACE: silent, impassive, stubbornly resistant.

                    SMITH
            If you had looked into his eyes as I have
            you'd know. He is dangerous. I tell you -

AMY stares into infinity and Smith's words become an
incomprehensible drone in the background.

108 INT. ISAAC FOSTER'S COTTAGE. DAY.   108

AMY; FOSTER - sullen; her mother, MARY - tight lipped; the
three SIBLINGS - tearful.

                    MARY FOSTER
            You should listen to Mr. and Mrs. Smith
            even if you won't listen to us. They care
            about you. They know what's best.

Amy, apparently deaf, comforts her little sister.

                    MARY
            We're already the talk of the parish.

                    FOSTER
            Well? It's not for the first time. We're   *
            the experts aren't we? This is the school   *
            for bloody scandal.   *

Mary flinches at her husband's cruelty. She strikes back.

                                              (CONTINUED)

> MARY
> It's a donkey's age since I expected
> aught of you as a husband, Isaac Foster,
> but you could try to be some kind of
> father to your children.

Isaac broods sullenly.

> MARY
> Isaac, please. Just tell her to stay away
> from him.

> FOSTER
> You've no right to tell her anything.

Mary strikes Isaac back in his deepest wound.

> MARY
> I should have stayed with your father.

Isaac slaps Mary across the face, looms again over her as she
cowers -- Amy grabs his wrist. Issac looks at her.   *

> AMY
> Father.

Isaac can't hold her gaze. His eyes drop. She lets go of him.
He looks up - finds Amy's eyes still on him.

> FOSTER
> Go on then. Go and have your way with
> your gypsy!   *

Amy walks out. Mary intercepts her at the door. She lowers
her voice so the children can't hear. Her eyes - darting the
odd furtive glance back in the room - plead with all the
fear of her own regret and suffering.

> MARY
> Amy? When I was your age I was foolish
> too. Do you understand?
>   (whispers)
> I was in love.

> AMY
> You and father were married late. I know.
> You were already expecting me but--

> MARY
> Amy! That madness in the blood is a
> trecherous thing! It is God's trick upon
> us women! You must --
>   (calms herself)
> I just don't want to see the same thing
> happen to you. It's not worth it, believe
> me. Please.

(CONTINUED)

108 CONTINUED: 108

AMY doesn't answer. She kisses Mary on the cheek then turns
and walks away.

As Mary watches her go something dies in her eyes.

109 EXT. NEW BARNS FARM. DAY.   109

SMITH, in a field, sees: YANKO walking down the road beyond
the dry-stone wall.

Smith grips his stick and strides over to the wall.

                    SMITH
          Oi!

Yanko stops by the wall. He is guarded but polite.

                    YANKO
          Good evening, sir.

A click of the heels, a small bow. The politeness infuriates
Smith even more.

                    SMITH
          It may not be my business to tell you how
          to live your life - fair enough. But if I
          find you about my property again I'll
          break your head for you.

SMITH backs off in fear as YANKO suddenly tosses his jacket
onto the stones and leaps up to stand atop the wall. His
black eyes sparkle down fiercely. He says nothing. Smith
continues to retreat.

                    SMITH
          And that's as fair a warning as you'll
          get!

Yanko watches Smith turn and walk away.

110 EXT. COLEBROOK - THE CHURCHYARD. DAY.   110

The bells are ringing for services.

Yanko walks toward the church spire down the road.

A long line of townspeople are queueing their way into the
church. Canon Van Stone welcomes them on the threshold. A
busy - circulating - chatter of nods, smiles and greetings.

As YANKO approaches a head turns here and there - and sees
him. More heads -- more hard faces. More.

As they turn their chatter and movement CEASES.

Yanko stops - frozen by:

                                                        (CONTINUED)

110 CONTINUED: 110

A long wall of SILENT STARING FACES. Amongst them: Vincent;
Mr. and Mrs. Finn; Preble; Thackery; Miss. Crotty and her
companion, MRS. RIGBY; Mrs. Smith; Widow Cree and her sons.
Children follow their parents cue. Van Stone.

Cold, silent, masks. Only the bell makes a sound.

YANKO watches - rooted to the spot as --

One by one each and every face turns away from him. The
people file swiftly into the church. The bell stops ringing.

YANKO is alone.

111 INT. NEW BARNS FARM - AMY'S ROOM. DAY. 111

AMY - dressed in her finery - but looking both melancholy and
anxious - paces up and down like a caged tiger, each time,
glancing down through the window.

She stops - and decides - and walks to the door.

112 EXT. THE HILL - THE THREE NORWAY PINES. DAY. 112

Amy runs up the hill to the wall. She looks over, hopefully,
towards --

The three pines. But YANKO is not there.

Amy runs back down the hill.

113 EXT. ST CHRISOPHER'S CHURCH. DAY. 113

Amy walks into the church.

114 INT. ST CHRISTOPHER'S CHURCH. DAY. 114

The church is empty except for -- VAN STONE -- putting out
candles on the altar. He sees AMY. He blinks - awkward and
ashamed. He wraps himself in what piety he can muster and
walks down the aisle towards her.

                    VAN STONE
          Amy. We haven't seen you here since your   *
          schooldays.

Amy doesn't answer. She looks around the church.

                    VAN STONE
          Your -- friend -- if that is the reason
          for your visit, did not attend the
          service.

AMY turns her back in him and walks out.

115   EXT. COLEBROOK POINT - THE MEMORIAL. DAY.   115

        YANKO stands in an almost trance-like state of despair. He is
        looking at --

        A squat, rough-hewn monument of fresh granite.

        AMY comes up behind him. She slips her hand into his.

                              YANKO
                    Amy!
                         (realizes)
                    I am -- Forgive me. I am out of the time
                    to be with you. I am --

        Amy smiles tenderly, puts a finger against his lips.

                              AMY
                    You are with me now.

                              YANKO
                    Their faces are - so hard. Their eyes -
                    like glass. I do not understand this. I
                    do not.

        He looks to her for an answer. Amy takes his hand.   *

                              AMY   *
                    I don't care to understand them.   *

                              YANKO   *
                    But we need, yes?   *

                              AMY   *
                         (shakes her head)   *
                    I eat with them, I work with them, but I   *
                    do not live with them. And I don't need   *
                    to understand them.   *

                              YANKO   *
                    How did you know I am here?   *

        Amy indicates the granite monument. Yanko is bewildered. Amy   *
        points to an inscription carved in the stone. Yanko looks at   *
        it -- then back to Amy. It's clear he can't understand the   *
        written words. Amy reads them for him.   *

                              AMY   *
                    'IN MEMORY OF THAT VALIANT COMPANY WHICH   *
                    BRAVED THE SEA, IN SEARCH OF A NEW WORLD,   *
                    AND DIED IN SIGHT OF THIS GROUND'   *

        Yanko appreciates the words, but doesn't grasp their   *
        significance.   *

                                                        (CONTINUED)

115   CONTINUED: 115

                         YANKO   *
              Good words, yes, I think. But it is for   *
              who? What - who - is dead?   *
                                                                          *
Amy looks at him.   *

                         AMY   *
              It's for the ship - your ship.   *

                         YANKO   *
              My ship?   *

A dawning horror.   *

                         YANKO   *
              My ship is not in Amerika?   *

Amy realises he did not know. Her heart aches for him.   *

                         AMY   *
              Your ship was swallowed up by the sea.   *
              No-one was left alive - except you.   *

                         YANKO   *
              Stephan? All the children, the--   *

                         AMY   *
              They're all here.   *

Yanko: a mass of emotions - grief, or, mystery, confusion -   *
assail him. He struggles. Amy puts her arm around his   *
waist.   *

                         AMY   *
              Don't be sad, my beauty. Come with me.   *

He looks at her, confused. She smiles mysteriously.   *

116   EXT. THE CLIFFS. DAY.   116

Amy and Yanko walk arm in arm along the cliffs. The sea roars
beneath them.

                         AMY
              You sing to the trees.

Yanko looks at her.

                         AMY
              The three tall pine trees on the hill.

Yanko is momentarily embarrassed.

(CONTINUED)

116 CONTINUED: 116

                         YANKO
                 Who said of me such thing?

                              AMY
                 No one. I watched you. In the winter.
                 Many times.

        Yanko stops, looks at her - captivated by the thought that
        she watched him. They have reached a steep path down the
        cliff towards the pounding surf.

        Amy smiles and skips down the path. Yanko follows.

117 EXT. THE ROAD. DAY.   117

        JACK VINCENT rides along on his grey horse. In the mid-
        distance he spots:

        AMY and YANKO, embracing. She takes his hand and they
        disappear over the cliff.

        Vincent wheels his horse around and set off apace.

118 EXT. THE CLIFF - THE CAVE. DAY.   118

        YANKO stands watching the sea crashing onto the rocks a few
        yards away. Spray cascades across his cheeks. He is no longer
        scared by it, but mesmerized.

        Behind him AMY - as if in a ritual - takes off her hat and
        boots. She places them on the rocks.

                              AMY
                 Yanko.

        He turns. Amy pulls aside the screen of weathered driftwood
        to reveal the dark entrance to the CAVE.

119 INT. THE CAVE. DAY.   119

        The light fades behind them as Amy, with sure steps, leads
        Yanko through a dark tunnel. She stops and crouches and
        reaches into a tar-caulked box. She opens a package wrapped
        in oiled paper: matches.

        Amy lights the wick of a lifeboat lamp - a heavy glass globe
        with a strong flame. She leads on.

120 INT. UNDERGROUND - THE RED CAVERN. DAY.   120

        AMY emerges from the tunnel. YANKO stops behind her.

                              AMY
                 This is where I live.

        Amy puts the lamp on a rock. The flame illuminates an
        underground FANTASIA.

                                                    (CONTINUED)

120 CONTINUED: 120

The time-sculpted walls of the vaunting CAVERN are shot
through with RED streaks of ore that give the reflected light
an ochre glow. And the walls and floor are littered - with a
beautiful haphazard logic - with exotic artifacts. Here: a
broken crate festooned with multi-patterned cotton cloths.
There: a strange ivory carving of a Siamese demon. Kegs,
furniture: drawers without chests; a chair, it's upholstery
rotted away; a hat stand, the glass floats. A cracked mirror
in a carved oak frame --

YANKO'S EYES reel back and forth, gaping.

Amy lights two more lamps - big brass- bound navigation lamps
- placed on outcrops of rock.

Yanko sees beside him -- a barrel of LIMES. He picks one up,
looks at it, mystified. He shows Amy the lime.

                    YANKO
          What is?

                    AMY
          It's a lime.

Amy puts the book down, takes a knife from the barrel and
cuts the lime in two, offers him half.

                    AMY
          They are good for the skin.

Yanko, tentatively, raises the lime and presses the inside
against -- his cheek. Amy bursts into delighted laughter.

                    AMY
          No! You eat them! See --

She bites into the lime and sucks. Yanko follows suit. His
eyes water and he gasps. Amy laughs again and drops her lime
in the barrel and --

Yanko watches, entranced, as --

Amy steps across her arena - with a grace and lightness of
step that no one has seen before. She plucks a whispering
length of yellow silk cloth from a copper-studded trunk and
drapes it around her herself, dramatically, and whirls and
reclines against a bale of wool like a siren of old. She
pulls a corner of the silk across her mouth - suddenly self-
conscious of her immodesty.

                    AMY
          Do you like my home?

                    YANKO
              (in wonder)
          These things - how did you get?

                                              (CONTINUED)

63.

120 CONTINUED: 120

> AMY
> I found them on the beach. They are the
> gifts of the sea. I never know when the
> gifts are going to come. But they are
> always beautiful.

She comes up to him and takes his hands.

> AMY
> You came from the sea.

Yanko looks at her - heart swelling.

Then Yanko starts to make music.

> YANKO
> La-la-la, la-la-la, lah--

A dark mountain waltz - his rich voice echoes from the walls.
And he dances, slowly at first, then faster, turning, moving
in graceful, turning steps through the flickering light. Not,
this time, the warrior's dance -- but the lover's.

Amy watches him - enchanted - as Yanko's throat trembles with
the soaring notes and his face fills with a joy both
melancholy and sublime. He holds out his hands -- and Amy
takes them.

Amy and Yanko dance.

121 INT. THE COACH AND HORSES. EVENING.   121

The Notables: PREBLE, THACKERY and JACK VINCENT, the latter
drunk - and bloated with secret knowledge. ISAAC FOSTER
brings a pint over to a nearby table.

> PREBLE
> I wouldn't want to lose my daughter to a
> character like that -

Thackery nudges him. Foster seems not to notice.

> VINCENT
> I expect now that they'll have to be wed.

At this Foster turns.

> FOSTER
> There's been no talk of marriage nor will
> there be any such. He's a fair hand with
> sheep but he's not fit for any girl to
> marry.

> PREBLE
> These foreigners behave very queerly with
> women, you know.

(CONTINUED)

>   VINCENT
>   Hark at the worldly wheelwright! Why
>   tha's never been further afield than
>   Truro market! What do you know about
>   foreigners - or women?
>
>   PREBLE
>   (hurt)
>   All I'm saying is that these gypsies know
>   how to take advantage. He's cast a
>   glamour over her. That's what they do.
>
>   VINCENT
>   Mind you - if they do wed - she won't
>   find out much that she isn't already
>   familiar with.

Isaac Foster stares Vincent in the eye.

>   FOSTER
>   What dost tha' mean by that, Jack
>   Vincent?
>
>   VINCENT
>   Tha'll miss the money too, I dare say.
>   The girl gives all her wages to her
>   mother, doesn't she?

Thackery senses trouble.

>   THACKERY
>   Take no notice, Isaac. Jack's got a right
>   mood on him tonight.

Foster shakes the hand off and stands up.

>   FOSTER
>   I want to know what it is that my Amy's
>   so 'familiar' with!

Vincent stares up at him brazenly.

>   VINCENT
>   All I'm saying is that things were seen.
>   Not speculations or imaginings. Things.
>   This very afternoon. Down near the old
>   wreckers cave. Things that leave no room
>   for doubt in the matter.
>
>   FOSTER
>   I'll teach thee a lesson, big as you are!

Foster grabs Vincent by the shirt front. Vincent rises,
towering, and wraps his hand round Foster's throat.   *

CLOSE ON: Thackery, who is looking out of the pub window.   *

                                                  (CONTINUED)

121 CONTINUED: 121

    HIS POV: Amy and Yanko walk down the street by the shore.   *

    Thackery dashes over and tries to part Foster and Vincent.   *

                  THACKERY   *
          Gentlemen! Gentlemen! Isn't it someone   *
          else needs teaching the lesson.   *

    Isaac looks at him.   *

122 EXT. COLEBROOK DOCK - AN ALLEYWAY. NIGHT.   122

    CLOSE -- A FIST smashes into someone's gut.   *

    AMY'S FACE: Tears streaming. She screams.   *

                    AMY   *
          No! No! Leave him alone!   *

    Amy is struggling - pinned - in Thackery's arms by the alley. *
    She can't see down the alley - only hear the sounds - of a   *
    savage beating. Punches, curses, gasps and moans.   *

    PREBLE stands at the mouth of the alley, looking down.   *
    from which some the sounds of a savage beating. Punches,   *
    curses, gasps and moans.   *

    In the alley: Vincent - bleeding from the nostrils has - has   *
    Yanko pinned by the arms while Issac Foster - white with   *
    rage, also bleeding from the mouth - punctuates his words   *
    with punches to Yanko's body.   *

                    FOSTER
          You really think you're it --
              (punch)
          DON'T you? Hob-nobbing with the bloody
          DOCTOR --
              (punch)
          Wining and dining with the SWAFFERS --
              (punch)
          Putting your filthy hands on my DAUGHTER.
              (punch)
    Punch. Isaac pauses for breath, staring at Yanko, pouring
    into him the bitterness he feels towards so much else.
    With what strength he has left Yanko spits a lump of bloody
    phlegm into Isaac's face. Isaac takes a step back; trembles.

122a EXT. COLEBROOK DOCK. NIGHT.   122a

    AMY reacts as: *

    Issac drags Yanko out of the alley and down the slipway to   *
    the sea. Issac doesn't even look at her as she shouts   *

(CONTINUED)

122a CONTINUED: 122a

                              AMY   *
                        Father! Father!   *

Thackery - holding Amy - looks increasingly uncomfortable.   *
His grip loosens. Amy breaks free, runs.   *

In the SEA: Issac pulls Yanko up, whispers in his ear.   *

                              FOSTER
                  You should've done yourself a favour and
                  stayed under witr the rest of 'em.

Foster pushes Yanko under again. Another splash, then - AMY   *
grabs hold of Foster's hair, pulls his head up. He looks at   *
her - at the horror and anger in her face - and something in   *
Foster's heart is pierced. His shoulders relax. He lets go   *
of Yanko, turns abruptly and wades away. Amy pulls Yanko to   *
his feet.   *

Amy pulls Yanko to his feet

123   EXT. KENNEDY'S HOUSE. NIGHT.   123

KENNEDY opens his door and looks down - with shock.

Amy supports a hunched figure, clutching his ribs, at the   *
foot of the steps. YANKO raises his face: his features are   *
bleeding and badly battered.   *

                              KENNEDY   *
                        Yanko! My dear fellow!   *

Kennedy takes his other arm. Yanko sways on his feet,   *
coughing violently. Kennedy and Amy helps him up the steps.   *

                              KENNEDY   *
                  Come along, now. Carefully, mind. Wait   *
                  for us in the parlour, Amy.   *

She starts to speak --   *

                              KENNEDY   *
                  Please, I must tend to him.   *

Amy closes her mouth. Kennedy takes Yanko inside.   *

124   INT. KENNEDY'S HOUSE - THE SURGERY. NIGHT.   124

YANKO sits with his ribs strapped up.

On the nearby table are bandages, lint, instruments, bottles
of alcohol and witchhazel. Kennedy is stitching a cut over
Yanko's left eye. Beneath his professional cool Kennedy is
white with outrage. He snips a suture.

                                                             (CONTINUED)

                    KENNEDY
          I can guess well enough who did this -
          but why?

                    YANKO
          They said I was to stay away. They said
          if I was to marry her, they would put me
          back into the sea...

                    KENNEDY
          Marry who?

                    YANKO
          Why, Amy.

                    KENNEDY
          Amy? Amy Foster - the Smiths' girl?

                    YANKO
          Yes. I have been -- walking with her. You
          did not know this?

                    KENNEDY
          The town gossips do not share their
          confidences with me - I'm glad to say.
          But why did you not tell me?

Yanko shuffles. He looks away from Kennedy's eyes.

                    YANKO
          It has not been time. And I -- I had
          fear.

Kennedy looks at him.

                    YANKO
          All people - the mask people - were
          against it. Against her, always, yes,
          always. And against me. I -- I did not
          want you to be against me.

                    KENNEDY
          Yanko, I would never be against you. You
          are my friend - my good friend.

But it's not quite that simple. Kennedy's anger evaporates in
complex emotions of his own. He turns away and busies himself
with a bottle of astringent.

                    KENNEDY
          Has she agreed to marry?

                    YANKO
          I have not asked. But I will.

                                                  (CONTINUED)

                         KENNEDY
               You're sure of what you are doing?

                         YANKO
               It is the wish of my heart.

Kennedy dabs at the sutured cut on Yanko's head.

                         KENNEDY
               I do not like to speak of things in which
               I am not expert - but you should be aware
               that Amy has always been a
               little...strange.

                         YANKO
               Srange? Explain me.

                         KENNEDY
               Her mother brought her to me when she was
               nine years old. Amy had been at the
               parish school for three years and yet had
               made not the slightest attempt to learn
               to read or write.

Yanko flinches involuntarily as Kennedy dabs his wound.

                         KENNEDY
               Almost done. However, I examined the
               child - she spoke not a word to me - but
               I could find no obvious cause for her -
               retardation. I presumed she was slow of
               mind - some form of childhood catatonia.
               Then the very next week - to the
               astonishment of all, including myself -
               she began to read and write. Just like
               that. And perfectly adequately too. She
               kept it up for just one month. Then she
               stopped. And as far as anyone knows she
               has picked up neither pen nor paper ever
               since.
                         (beat)
               I am mystified by Amy - I admit it. As a
               scientist, mystery to me is the fabric of
               our universe - but to the townsfolk it is
               something to be feared.

Yanko - studying Kennedy's face rather than his words -
interrupts him.

                         YANKO
               You are not happy for me.

Kennedy looks at Yanko for a long moment. And Kennedy
realizes in himself - perhaps for the first time - how much
Yanko's friendship means to him - and what a true friend
should do. Kennedy smiles.

                                              (CONTINUED)

                    KENNEDY
          I am always happy to see a friend follow
          'the wish of his heart'.

                    YANKO
          You are not angry?

                    KENNEDY
          No.

                    YANKO
          I have found my true gold.

                    KENNEDY
          Then you must hold onto it.

Yanko squeezes Kennedy's arm. His face becomes troubled.

                    YANKO
          I need the blessing of a wise man - a
          father.

                    KENNEDY
          If it is in my power to give it - I would
          do so most freely.

                    YANKO
                (shaking his head)
          You are my friend. It is not correct.

YANKO has an idea - it scares him, but he feels hope.

                    YANKO
          Mr. Swaffer. I will ask him. Yes?

                    KENNEDY
                (wryly)
          Old Swaffer is capable of anything. But
          you must rest here until you are fit.
          Come along, I'll show you to your room.

                    YANKO   *
          Where is Amy.   *

124A INT. KENNEDYS WAITING ROOM. NIGHT.   124A*

                    KENNEDY   *
          You inhaled a lot of sea water. Your
          lungs will be vulnerable. I strongly   *
          advise that you rest here.   *

Kennedy is stunned to see Amy stood exactly where she left   *
him.   *

                                        (CONTINUED)

124A CONTINUED: 124A

                          AMY   *
               I'll take him home.   *

                          KENNEDY   *
               To Swaffers? But it's miles, really, Amy,   *
               you must --   *

                          AMY   *
               I'll care for him.   *

     Kennedy sees the resolution in her eyes. He is rather   *
     affronted that his judgement is being ignored. He looks at   *
     Yanko. He sees that Yanko wants to go too.   *

                          YANKO   *
               Kennedy, thank you for your care. You have   *
               made me well.   *

     Kennedy sighs, and holds his palm towards the door.   *

                          KENNEDY   *
               Very well.   *

124B EXT. KENNEDYS HOUSE . NIGHT.   124B*

     Kennedy watches from the steps as Amy and Yanko walk off into   *
     the night. Then his eyes focus elsewhere -- and harden into   *
     an altogether grimmer anger.   *

     125 - OMITTED   *

     126 - OMITTED   *

127 INT. THE COACH AND HORSES. NIGHT.   127

     Vincent, Thackery, Preble and Isaac Foster. Drunk.

     The DOOR crashes open. Heads turn from bar and tables.

     KENNEDY stands on the threshold, holding his cane. He
     searches out the Notables - Vincent, Thackery, Preble. He
     takes his hat off. As Kennedy walks over they shuffle and
     stare into their beer.

     Kennedy stops at Foster - alone at his table.

                          KENNEDY
               Foster? I excuse you - just - from what I
               am about to say because of your familial
               involvement. But the rest of you?

     He turns on the Notables - his eyes blazing with anger.

                          KENNEDY
               The rest of you all saw the bodies of
               that man's tragic companions - laid out
               in their hundreds! - by the very church
                          (MORE)

                                                          (CONTINUED)

127 CONTINUED: 127

                        KENNEDY (cont'd)
          in which you all so piously pretend to
          pray.

Kennedy's knuckles whiten on his cane.

                        KENNEDY
          You have disgraced this community. You
          have disgraced me, personally.

He looks each of them in the face. They avoid his gaze.

                        KENNEDY
          And you are a disgrace to yourselves.

Kennedy's lip curls with disgust. He restrains himself.

                        KENNEDY
          And bear in mind - as you swill your ale
          and tell your filthy tales - that to take
          part in the violence of the mob is as low
          as any man - who calls himself a man -
          can fall.

A heavy silence. Thackery and Preble are cowed -- but Vincent
- with drunken belligerence - starts to rise.

                        VINCENT
          I've had enough of this.

Kennedy sweeps his cane across the table. The Notables recoil
as they are showered with broken glass and beer. Vincent
collapses, floundering and spluttering, back into his chair.
He wheezes as the tip of Kennedy's cane jams into his throat.
His eyes bulge up at KENNEDY.

                        KENNEDY
          Do not threaten me, blacksmith. For if it
          were not at odds with my vocation, I
          would take you outside and treat you to
          the thrashing you so richly deserve.

Kennedy withdraws his cane. Vincent gasps.

Kennedy glances around at the faces gaping at him from all
about the room. Kennedy claps his hat back on.

                        KENNEDY
          Goodnight, 'gentlemen'.

Kennedy strides out.

128 EXT. THE COACH AND HORSES. NIGHT.   128

Kennedy pauses - as if mildly astonished at his own
performance. He straightens his hat. He strides away.

129   EXT. THE BEACH. NIGHT.   129

       Waves foam up the beach by the CAVE. The screen is open.

130   INT. THE CAVE. NIGHT.   130

       AMY helps YANKO across the floor of the cavern into the
       shadows -- into the rear. Yanko, looking down, stops. They
       are standing on the edge of --

       AN UNDERGROUND POOL: its glassy surface glitters jet black in
       the soft light. Here and there wisps of STEAM rise from the
       surface.

                          AMY
                 It is warm. It will heal you.

       Yanko looks at her - a little anxiously. Amy peels his jacket
       off. His shirt.

                          AMY
                 Don't be afraid.

       AMY climbs into the pool and stands waist deep. She holds out
       her hands. Yanko steps down into the water. Amy cradles him
       in her arms in the soft water. They look at each other.

       Yanko stands up to face her. Her dress clings to her body.
       Tentatively - her hands touch his chest. A great passion
       seizes them. Amy slips her dress down.

       For a moment they are both shocked at themselves.

       They kiss.

       Their hands and mouths discover each other's flesh. Her neck.
       His shoulder. His chest. Her breast.

131   THE SAME -- LATER.   131

       Amy and Yanko make love on the bale of wool amongst the
       lamplit sea treasures of the cavern.

132   THE SAME - LATER.   132

       Amy and Yanko lie each others arms in the flickering ochre
       light. Amy plays with his hair. Yanko looks at her.

                          YANKO
                 Will you be married with me, Amy Foster?

       Amy looks into his face. She is intensely moved.

                          AMY
                 Yes, I will. And I will love you until   *
                 the end of the world.

133   OMITTED   133

134   EXT. SWAFFER'S FARMHOUSE. DAY.   134

       YANKO, his face still bruised and stitched, walks to the
       house. He straightens his clothes -- knocks on the door.

       SWAFFER opens it and wordlessly takes in Yanko's dress, his
       battered face.

135   INT. SWAFFER'S PARLOUR. DAY.   135

       SWAFFER stands by MISS. SWAFFER in her chair.

       YANKO is in the middle of his plea. He swallows.

                         YANKO
             And so - Sir and Miss - I ask you to be
             given your permission to marry Miss Amy
             Foster.

       There is a long silence. Yanko's eyes flit from one to the
       other. Then Swaffer, in his usual deliberate manner, nods in
       dismissal.

       Yanko bows and leaves.

       Swaffer turns to Miss Swaffer and raises an eyebrow.

                         MISS SWAFFER
             Well. He won't get any other girl to
             marry him.

       Her eyes narrow as if with an idea. She looks at Swaffer.

                         MISS SWAFFER
             Go to Darnford, today, and ask my good
             brother-in-law if he will pay us a visit.

       Swaffer's other brow rises level with the first. Without
       questioning her, he walks for the door.

135a   EXT. COLEBROOK HIGH STREET. DAY.   135a

       MARY FOSTER, in comparatively shabby clothes, walks with her
       children, loaded with shopping baskets of staples. She looks
       up as MISS CROTTY, MRS. FINN and MISS. RIGBY flock across the
       street towards her. Crotty smiles with sanctimonious concern

                         MISS. CROTTY
             Hello, Mary, dear. How are the children?

                         MARY FOSTER
             They're well enough, thank you.

(CONTINUED)

135a CONTINUED: 135a

                         MISS. CROTTY
                We wouldn't want you to think we were
                interfering in matters that don't concern
                us, but -- there's been talk in the
                parish. About your Amy.

Mary colours with a mixture of shame and anger.

                         MRS. FINN
                She's been seen, well --
                     (struggles to find a
                     respectable word)

                         MRS. RIGBY
                'Consorting'.

                         MRS. FINN
                Yes, consorting let us say, with that vile gypsy.   *

                         MISS. CROTTY
                We thought it was only right that you
                should know.

        MARY: terribly humiliated.

136   EXT. SWAFFER'S YARD. DAY.   136

        YANKO paces in an agony of uncertainty. He wheels as --

        Swaffer emerges from the house and - without so much as a
        glance - walks to the coach house.

137   THE SAME -- SHORTLY.   137

        YANKO - even more agitated - looks up as --

        SWAFFER rolls out on his cart and -- sweeps on past him.

138   EXT. THE FIELDS. DAY.   138

        YANKO strides across the meadow towards NEW BARNS FARM.

        YANKO peers over a wall into Smith's yard -- sees:

        ISAAC and MARY FOSTER entering the yard.

        YANKO, frustrated, pulls back into the field.

139   EXT. SMITH'S YARD. DAY.   139

        Mary - white lipped - and Isaac - reluctant - cross the yard
        towards the farmhouse.

        Mary knocks on the kitchen door.

140   INT. NEW BARNS - THE KITCHEN. DAY.   140

AMY carries a tray of crockery to the sink. MRS. SMITH goes
to answer the door.

AMY - washing up - hears --

                    MRS. SMITH
            Mary? Isaac? Well. Please, come in.

AMY turns, sees: ISAAC and MARY.

Amy turns back to the sink.

MARY FOSTER almost charges in past the bewildered Mrs. Smith.
ISAAC shuffles in after her.

                    FOSTER
            Excuse us for bothering you at this hour,
            Mrs. Smith, we won't keep you - Mary just
            needs to have a word with --

                    MARY
            AMY!

MARY stands a few feet behind Amy, shaking with rage.

Slowly, AMY turns and looks at her mother.

                    MARY
            You're coming home with us this instant.

AMY looks at her mother's face - and sees the grief of
decades stored there, now pouring out towards her. Amy shakes
her head and turns away. MARY reaches out and pulls Amy
around by her shoulder.

                    MARY
            Do you hear me?

                    AMY
            No.

Mary SLAPS Amy across the face, spinning her head aside.

Mrs. Smith cries out.

AMY straightens her head and looks her mother in the eye.

FOSTER rushes over and pulls Mary away.

                    FOSTER
            Mary! That's enough. Leave her be.

Mary shrugs Isaac's hands off and turns from Amy to him - her
eyes wild in a moment of supreme irony, supreme agony,
supreme revenge. In a terrible whisper:

                                            (CONTINUED)

140   CONTINUED: 140

                              MARY
                    Leave her be?

She turns - propelled into an irrevocable abyss - to AMY.

                              MARY
                    I was carrying you before he ever laid
                    hands on me.
                         (indicates Isaac)
                    Carrying you for his father. I slaved for
                    them like you slave for this lot.

She waves a derisive hand at --

Mrs. Smith - white-faced, clutching Mr. Smith's arm.

                              MARY
                    And they both had their fill - the father
                    and the son.

Mary's face trembles at the enormity of her life.

                              MARY   *
                    He isn't your father. Do you understand?   *
                    He's your brother.   *
                         (self-disgust)   *
                    Your half-brother.   *

Amy looks at Issac, he turns away. Amy looks back at Mary
without speaking.

                              MARY
                    See? Not a word. Not a tear.

Mary is shaking. She flings a finger at Amy.

                              MARY
                    Bad you were conceived and bad you've
                    remained!

AMY looks at Mary for a moment longer. Then turns back to the
window.

In her eyes we see: immense pain.

Behind her, Mary starts sobbing. Isaac takes Mary by the
shoulders and leads her, weeping, to the door - and out.

Mr. Smith closes the door after them. He looks at his wife.
They both look at:

Amy's back, bent over the sink, washing cups.

Mrs. Smith walks out of the kitchen, motioning with her head
for Smith to follow. He lingers.

(CONTINUED)

140 CONTINUED: 140

                          SMITH
                Amy? If you want to take a few days off,
                well, I'll make sure it's alright with
                the Missis.

Amy, her back to him, doesn't react.

                          SMITH
                        (gently)
                Did you hear me, girl?

                          AMY
                Yes, sir. Thank you, sir.

Smith nods at her back and leaves.

As she hears the door close, Amy's tears tumble silently onto
the cup in her hands. The cup falls into the water. Amy's
hands grip the edge of the sink.

Amy rips her apron off and stumbles towards the door.

141 EXT. NEW BARNS - THE YARD. DAY.   141

YANKO sees: Isaac lead the sobbing Mary out of the yard.
They see him -- and stare at him with a hatred so intense he
is almost hypnotized. Issac lurches towards him.   *

                          FOSTER   *
                I'll swing for you, you filth.   *

Mary pulls him back.   *

                          FOSTER   *
                Why did you have to come here with your   *
                dirty gyppo ways? We were alright till   *
                you showed up. We were happy --   *

                          MARY   *
                Issac, plesae.   *

He turns to look at her. Their eyes: *

                          MARY   *
                The children are on their own.   *

Issac softens - and perhaps this is the first moment of   *
connection they have felt in many years. Issac takes her arm.   *

Yanko - terribly disturbed, upset - watches them disappear -   *
then jumps from the wall into the yard.   *

142 EXT. NEW BARNS - THE SHEDS - SHORTLY.   142

Yanko stands waiting at the open door to the miling sheds -
above which is Amy's room. Smith sticks his head out of Amy's
bedroom window and and calls down to Yanko.

                                              (CONTINUED)

142   CONTINUED: 142

                    SMITH
              Amy's not here. Maybe she went back with
              her parents after all ---

Yanko is already sprinting across the yard.

143   EXT. THE HILLS. EVENING.   143

AMY runs across the fields in the darkness.

144   EXT. THE CLIFFS. EVENING.   144

A POV: AMY'S SILHOUETTE running along the distant cliff top
in the moonlight.

                    PREBLE (O.S.)
              Christ. I thought Foster said she'd be at
              the Smiths all night.

The POV belongs to VINCENT and PREBLE, sitting on a cart on
the road. Vincent leans his face into Preble's.

                    VINCENT
              We've done the necessary. Just remember
              that no one said naught to nobody about
              nothing.

145   EXT. THE MOORS. EVENING.   145

YANKO -- running.

146   EXT. THE CLIFFS. EVENING.   146

AMY runs pell mell through the long grass. Suddenly she
reacts - throws herself down to stop herself -- lands on her
knees right at -- THE EDGE of the cliff.

Below her is the smoking thunder of the SEA.

147   EXT. THE CLIFF. NIGHT.   147

AMY clambers down the steep rocky path to the beach.

THE BEACH: Amy runs forward - then STOPS.

The CAVE: the screen of driftwood has been pulled aside from
the entrance. Faint LIGHT flickers in the tunnel.

AMY rushes in.

148   INT. THE TUNNEL - THE CAVERN. EVENING.   148

As Amy hurries down the tunnel the light gets brighter.
Fierce crackling sounds. AMY stops dead at the end. Yellow
light dances across the horror on her face.

                                                    (CONTINUED)

148 CONTINUED: 148

Her fantasia is ABLAZE.

All her treasure have been heaped together and set alight.
The crates and trunks - burning. The wool - burning. The
spilled limes - scorching, blackening, shrivelling. The
furniture, the sheets of cloth flapping in the updraft -- all
of it burning.

AMY: tears tumble silently down her face. With terrifying
deliberation - she walks into the raging cavern and towards
the bonfire. Roars and crackles. The fire shifts:

The cracked MIRROR slips down the pyre, its frame blazing.
Amy's reflection looks back at her.

                    AMY
              Bad you were conceived. And bad you've
              remained.

149 EXT. THE BEACH. EVENING.   149

YANKO plunges, helter-skelter down the rocky path and sprints
across the beach.

He plunges into the cave.

150 INT. THE TUNNEL - THE CAVE. NIGHT.   150

Yanko hears the roar of the flames. He plunges forward.

                    YANKO
              AMY! AMY FOSTER!

YANKO explodes from the tunnel, reels from the heat:

AMY - stands perilously close to the fire.

Yanko shouts above the roaring inferno.

                    YANKO
              AMY!

Amy turns - sees him running towards her. She doesn't realize
how close the fire is and -- her skirt whooshes up in FLAMES.

Yanko charges across the cavern and -- sweeps her into his
arms and -- runs past the blaze towards --

151 THE UNDERGROUND POOL.   151

Yanko and Amy - flames billowing - plunge into the water.

YANKO flounders in the water, struggles to his feet --

AMY is already standing - unharmed- transfixed by the blaze
in the cavern. Yanko wades towards her.

                                              (CONTINUED)

151 CONTINUED: 151

        She turns to him - and suddenly the fire doesn't matter. She   *
        touches his face. She cries, softly - smiles. Yanko takes her   *
        in his arms. They cling to each other.   *

        Wrapped in each other arms, they stand watching the fire.

152 EXT. THE BEACH - THE CLIFF. DAWN.   152

        Above the pounding surf -- two figures climb the steep path
        up the cliff face.

153 EXT. THE CLIFF ROAD. DAY.   153

        Amy and Yanko - scorched and ragged and bruised - walk hand
        in hand in downcast silence.

        They turn at the sound of cartwheels on the road.

        It's SWAFFER in his two wheeler. He pulls over.

                        SWAFFER
                I've been looking for you.

        Swaffer looks - with the appearance of mild interest - at
        their fire-ravaged clothes.

                        SWAFFER
                Correct me if I'm wrong, but isn't that
                the only decent suit you own?

        YANKO is too bewildered by the question to answer.

                        SWAFFER
                I suppose we'll just have to fit you out
                with another. That one certainly won't
                do.

        Yanko and Amy look at each other. It is such a relief to have
        someone more crazed than they are that - they smile.

                        SWAFFER
                Jump on board, then. You too, Miss
                Foster.

        The cart clatters off with Amy and Yanko clinging on.

154 EXT. TALFOURD HILL. DAY.   154

        The cart drives along the hill road. They approach:

        A small stone COTTAGE with diamond windows and climbing roses
        round the door trellis. Swaffer stops the cart outside, next
        to a second - much larger - carriage.

                                                            (CONTINUED)

154 CONTINUED: 154

                         SWAFFER
                    Well? Get down.

Yanko helps Amy down. They look at each other again - neither
of them know what is going on. Amy looks over Yanko's
shoulder. He turns to follow her gaze towards the cottage. To
his astonishment he sees:

MISS SWAFFER sitting in the doorway at the top of a board
placed up to the threshold as a ramp. There is a gleam in her
grey eyes. She wheels herself away into the interior.

155 INT. THE COTTAGE. DAY.   155

A simple room, barely furnished. Present: Miss Swaffer; and
Mrs. WILLCOX, holding baby BERTHA. In the middle: an oilcloth
table covered with a number of documents. Standing behind the
table is MR. WILLCOX. He beams as:

AMY and YANKO enter.

                         WILLCOX
                    My goodness - you look like you've come
                    from the wars.

156 THE SAME - LATER.   156

YANKO'S FACE as his eyes rove uncomprehendingly over a sheet
of vellum. We see the words, elegantly inscribed:

                         WILLCOX
                    "In consideration of saving the life
                    of my beloved grandchild Bertha Willcox."

YANKO looks up from the document: he can't understand. Amy,
reading it beside him, suddenly looks up and around the room.
She walks towards the window.

                         YANKO
                       (to Willcox)
                    Please...

                         WILLCOX
                    My father-in-law - Mr. Swaffer, here -
                    has asked me to legally expedite this
                    deed of realty. And I can say in all
                    truth that no task in my career has ever
                    given me greater pleasure.

Yanko remains uncertain whether or not he is in trouble.
Willcox looks at Swaffer, who nods.

                         WILLCOX
                    What this means is that this cottage, and
                    the apportioned acre of land, have been
                    made over to you in absolute property,
                    without limit of time, and with full and
                    proper rights of ownership --

                                              (CONTINUED)

156 CONTINUED: 156

YANKO can't believe what he thinks he's hearing.

                         YANKO
              Please...

His eyes fall on Miss Swaffer, sitting by the fireplace.

                         MISS SWAFFER
              The cottage is YOURS! And the land too!
              Now can we all please go home?

YANKO'S FACE: struggling. He looks across at AMY.

AMY, her back towards him, is looking out of the window.

Her FACE: looking out at --

THE SEA -- swirling blue at the foot of the hill.

Amy turns to Yanko their eyes meet. She walks across the
room. Yanko rushes to her and clasps her to his chest, his
eyes close as he holds her. He opens them and sees:

WILLCOX - beaming with delight. Then: SWAFFER, rubbing his
upper lip to conceal his own pleasure.

MISS SWAFFER, appalled by these displays, wheels herself
towards the door.

YANKO rushes over and grabs Swaffer's hand. He so moved he is
afraid to speak.

                         YANKO
              Please. Sir. Thank you.

Swaffer shakes his head.

                         SWAFFER
              Don't thank me. I would never have
              thought of it.

Swaffer nods towards the escaping Miss Swaffer.

                         SWAFFER
              It was the daughter's idea.

Amy rushes over and intercepts Miss Swaffer at the door.
Their eyes meet.

                         AMY
              Thank you.

Miss Swaffer pauses; then she waves her hand dismissively --
and sternly wheels herself out and away down the ramp.

157   EXT. COLEBROOK - ST. CHRISTOPHER'S CHURCH. DAY.   157

The Church stands quietly amongst the trees.

KENNEDY'S PHAETON arrives at breakneck speed and clatters to
a halt. KENNEDY - looking dizzy from the journey- clambers
down. YANKO leaps from the driver's seat.

YANKO - anxious and proud in a borrowed dark suit - looks at
Kennedy. Kennedy smiles proudly.

                    KENNEDY
          Well? No power on earth can stop you now.

Kennedy produces a gold ring from his waistcoat, smiles.

                    KENNEDY
          And I am a very reliable second.

158   INT. ST. CHRISTOPHER'S CHURCH - THE SACRISTY. DAY.   158

A small group: KENNEDY, SWAFFER, MISS SWAFFER, MR. SMITH,
CANON VAN STONE, AMY FOSTER, YANKO. Van Stone takes down a
large tome - THE MARRIAGE REGISTER - and opens it on a desk.

Van Stone writes the name in the book: YANKO GOORALL.

Van Stone hands him the pen. Yanko looks at Kennedy.

Kennedy smiles and nods.

Yanko looks at AMY - in her best grey dress and green ribbon
she looks heart-breakingly lovely. Her eyes are full. Yanko
bends over the register.

THE REGISTER: in the canon's handwriting -

Yanko Gooral -- Amy Foster

YANKO'S HAND: shaking as he signs -- with an X.

YANKO straightens. He offers the pen to AMY.

AMY's hand, signing her name:

Amy Foster.

159   EXT. THE BEACH. DAY.   159

Amy - her arm around Yanko's waist, his around her shoulders
- and Yanko walk the deserted beach. A rare moment of
tranquility fulfilled. They stop, look out to:

The glittering immensity of the SEA.

160   EXT. TALFOURD HILL. NIGHT.   160

      The Cottage: amber light glows from the window.

161   OMITTED   161

162   EXT. NEW BARNS FARM. DAY.   162

      Amy comes from the kitchen carrying a single suitcase. Yanko
      - waiting outside - takes it from her. The SMITHS appear on
      the doorstep - they are awkward - but sad at her leaving.

                        SMITH
                  Mind that slave-driver Swaffer doesn't
                  take advantage now. And come and see us
                  from time to time.

      Mrs. Smith manages a nervous wave - then disappears inside.

                        SMITH
                     (unconvincingly)
                  Don't mind the missis. She's just sad to
                  see you go.

                        AMY
                  Thank you, Mr. Smith.

      Amy turns. She and Yanko walk away.

163   EXT. SWAFFER'S FIELD. DAY.   163

      YANKO - sweating and begrimed - stacks and bales hay.

164   INT. SWAFFER'S FARMOUSE. DAY.   164

      Under Miss Swaffer's watchful eye Amy cleans the kitchen.

165   EXT. TALFOURD HILL - THE ROAD. DUSK.   165

      Amy and Yanko - tired but happy - climb the hill to their
      cottage arm in arm.

166   EXT. COLEBROOK - THE MAIN STREET. DAY.   166

      AMY and YANKO walk arm in arm down the street. On the
      pavement ahead of them:

      MRS. FINN shudders and crosses the street to avoid them.

167   INT. THE CAVE. DAY.   167

      Amy and Yanko - in good spirits - are cleaning out the cavern
      and salvaging what little they can.

      Yanko shows her -- a charred LIME. He rubs it on his face.
      They laugh. Yanko smears charcoal on her nose.

167a INT. THE BEDROOM. NIGHT.   167a

    YANKO'S HEAD lies pillowed on Amy's breast. AMY strokes his
hair. He looks up at her, smiles.

> YANKO
> You are happy with me?

> AMY
> I could not be more happy.

Yanko looks off into space.

> YANKO
> My family too. My father, he will know my
> happiness. He keeps me in his inmost
> heart - always - and so he will know.

As he speaks he cannot see: AMY'S FACE - the sudden sadness
in her eyes as she thinks of her own family..

> YANKO
> Yes - my father will know of my love for
> you, even though he is very far.

As he turns to her, Amy hides her sadness and smiles.

> AMY
> And of mine for you.

> YANKO
> Yes! Yes - it is so.

He lifts his face to hers and they kiss.

Amy and Yanko make love.

168 EXT. COLEBROOK - THE SURGERY. DAY.   168

AMY and YANKO entering Kennedy's surgery.

169 INT. KENNEDY'S SURGERY - WAITING ROOM. DAY.   169

Three long worn-leather benches. Two of the rear benches are
full of taciturn townsfolk: murmurs; sour glances cast at:

YANKO and AMY - who have the front bench - conspicuously - to
themselves.

CLOSE ON: Mrs. Finn and Mrs. Rigby, conversing in whispers.

> MRS. RIGBY
> Well they both look well enough. I
> wounder what's the matter.

169 CONTINUED: 169

> MRS. FINN
> I'll bet she's - you know --
>   (mouths silently)
> Expecting.

> MRS. RIGBY
>   (just a bit too loudly)
> No! God preserve us!

Yanko - sensing more than understanding the murmurs -
shuffles on the bench. Amy, by contrast, turns in her seat
and stares directly at:

Finn and Rigby - who flutter their eyelashes and stare
straight ahead.

The door opens: Kennedy takes in the scene. His brows darken
- then one brow rises sardonically.

> KENNEDY
> Mrs. Rigby - what a surprise. Perhaps we
> should have a bed installed for you!

A scandalized gasp from the gathered. Kennedy - a twinkle in
his eye - beckons Amy and Yanko into his surgery.

170 INT. KENNEDY'S CONSULTING ROOM. DAY.   170

AMY sits with her hand on her belly. She looks at Yanko.
Yanko looks at Kennedy.

Kennedy smiles.

171 EXT. AMY'S COTTAGE. NIGHT.   171

Lights burn in the windows.

Yanko paces anxiously up and down outside the cottage.

172 OMITTED   172

173 INT. AMY'S COTTAGE. NIGHT.   173

AMY sits up in bed. A baby - not yet washed, with a shock of
moist black hair - suckles at her breast.

KENNEDY looks down on them. He is moved.

> KENNEDY
> Well, Amy. Now you have two fine men to
> look after you.

She looks at him. He smiles.

(CONTINUED)

173 CONTINUED: 173

                         KENNEDY
              You'll look after them, won't you?

                         AMY
              Yes, sir.

174 EXT. THE COTTAGE. NIGHT.   174

     Yanko rushes up as Kennedy appears in the doorway.

                         KENNEDY
              You now have a son - with almost as much
              hair as you have.

     Kennedy is startled as Yanko claps his arms round him and
     hugs him to his chest. To cover his own emotion --

                         KENNEDY
              I think they're waiting for you.

     Yanko lets go. Kennedy watches him disappear inside. Then
     collects himself and leaves.

175 INT. THE COTTAGE. NIGHT.   175

     YANKO holds the swaddles baby in awe. He looks at Amy - he
     bends and kisses her. He's speechless.

                         AMY
              He told me he wants to see the sea. Will
              you show him for me?

     Yanko swells inside.

176 EXT. AMY'S COTTAGE. DAWN.   176

     Kennedy has walked down the path to his carriage. He puts his
     bag in, climbs up, then turns and looks back as --

     The cottage door opens and -- YANKO appears on the threshold.
     Swaddled in his arms is A BABY.

     He appears almost in a trance as he stares at it and...

     A strain of music begins - mandolin, accordian and fiddle -
     the stirring sounds of his own mountains. He steps outside
     into the garden. The music swells.

     Slowly - the baby held in his arms - Yanko starts to DANCE.

     KENNEDY - moved. Gently, he urges his horses into motion.

     And YANKO dances and dances -- and dances. The music swirls
     and soars.

     VOICES join in - in a glorious celebration --

177 INT. A BARN IN THE CARPATHIAN MOUNTAINS. NIGHT.   177

THE CELEBRATION: the music swirling, friendly faces. YANKO
dancing amongst them with the BABY. He sees:

His BROTHERS - singing and smiling --

His mother, IRYNA, weeping with joy, then --

His father - NIKOLAS - proud. NIKOLAS opens his arms and
holds them out. Yanko's voice is heard - as was his father's
when he said farewell.

>   YANKO (V.O.)
>   I have a man! A strong man! He will sing
>   the songs of my heart. He will walk the
>   earth beside me. And one day I will teach
>   him how to dance!

And YANKO puts the babe in his father's arms.

178 EXT. TALFOURD HILL. DAWN.   178

YANKO'S FACE: streaming with tears as he walks towards...

The softly murmuming SEA.

YANKO holds HIS SON out towards the sea. A penetrating
sadness infiltrates the music.

AT THE WINDOW of the cottage: AMY'S FACE - full of love -
watches from behind the glass as:

YANKO dances against the backcloth of the moonlit sea. He
turns and sees her. He raises the infant towards her.

Close on AMY'S FACE: her eyes full with pride.

                                                    FADE TO

    179 - OMITTED

180 INT. AMY'S BEDROOM. NIGHT.   180

AMY lies in bed. She turns.

By the bed is a wickerwork cradle. YANKO kneels beside the
cradle murmuring to the child.

>   YANKO
>   I would like to teach Stefan my tongue -
>   my language. I would like that - to talk
>   with him.

He is uncertain of her reaction.

                                                    (CONTINUED)

89.

180 CONTINUED: 180

                         YANKO
              You would like that also?

                         AMY
              There is nothing you could teach him that
              I would not like.

Yanko beams, delighted.

                         YANKO
              Perhaps I teach you too!

Amy smiles. Yanko bends over the babe.

                         YANKO
              Stefan. Miy malen'kiy. Miy malen'kiy.
                    (in English
              We are the lucky ones.

181 EXT. COLEBROOK - THE HIGH STREET. DAY.   181

AMY walks down the high street. In one arm she carries baby
Stefan. In the other a loaded basket. Her attitude is one of
keeping herself to herself.

She stops outside the haberdashers and sets her basket down.
She looks in the window at the colourful array. She points
out the colours for the baby, murmuring to him.

                         BOY'S VOICE (O.S.)
              It's a bastard, him, that baby.

A chorus of daring sniggers and giggles. Amy turns.

A cocky group of boys - five or six of them - stand in a
gawping grinning semi-circle around Amy.

Amy stares at them, briefly, then turns away.

                         BOY
                    (showing off to his pals)
              It is. It's a bastard.

More giggles - at a slur they are unlikely to understand the
meaning of. Amy turns.

                         AMY
              Go away.

Stefan starts crying in her arm. Amy holds him tighter.

                         BOY
              I heard my dad say so. It's a bastard.

(CONTINUED)

181   CONTINUED: 181

                              AMY
                    Go away!

The Boy - losing face - suddenly darts forwards, fingers
reaching into his mouth to pull a face at the baby, tongue
gargling...

In a flash Amy's hand strikes out and lands a stinging slap
on the boy's cheek. The boy staggers back in shock.

Silence.

The boy starts bawling his eyes out.

Amy starts to walk away. She stops as MISS CROTTY comes out
of the butcher's shop to investigate - she recoils from the
sight of Amy. THACKERY emerges too.

                              THACKERY
                    What's going on here, then?

A babbling chorus of accusations arise from the boys.

                              MISS CROTTY
                    Look at that poor baby!

                              AMY
                    NEVER come near my baby again! Any of   *
                    you!   *

They all stare at her in silence.

Amy pushes her way past Miss Crotty and through the boys and
walks away down the street.

All along the street silent faces turn to watch her go.

182   INT. AMY AND YANKO'S COTTAGE. EVENING.   182

The door opens and Yanko enters, smiling. He looks across the
room, sees:

Amy, sitting hunched over the baby with her back to him.

                              YANKO
                    Amy?

She doesn't answer. Yanko goes over. Amy is crying silently.

                              YANKO
                    What is wrong? What has happened?

Yanko puts his arms around her.

183   EXT. A FOOTPATH ON THE HILL. DAY.   183

YANKO sits staring out at the sea. He is whittling - angrily
- on a piece of wood. He looks tired; a little pale. He
coughs a bit chesty - and hawks up phlegm; spits. Then:

> KENNEDY
> Yanko?

Yanko turns and sees Kennedy on his chesnut.

Kennedy dismounts and sits next to him. Yanko continues
cutting the wood. Kennedy notes his mood.

> KENNEDY
> It seems a good while since you called on
> me.

For a moment Yanko is reluctant to speak. He throws the piece
of wood away; snaps his knife shut. He looks back at Kennedy.

> YANKO
> I pay my way. I work my work. I take
> nothing. Why, then, still the hating?

> KENNEDY
> Because you come from far away.   *

> YANKO   *
> Everyone comes from somewhere.   *

> KENNEDY
> It seems without sense, I know. But to
> them you are strange. You are different.
> And in your difference they sense the
> shadow - the spectre - of their own
> otherness - the unknown that they fear
> inside themselves. It forms a gulf
> between you and them that can never be
> bridged.

> YANKO
> I do not understand. But for me - I
> accept. I am strong. But for Amy and our
> boy - I do not accept.

> KENNEDY
> Amy is different too.

> YANKO
> And my boy? Kennedy, I would like, when
> he is a man, to talk with me in my own
> tongue. Is that a bad thing?

>   KENNEDY
>   It seems natural enough.

>   YANKO
>   But I don't want that it should harm him.
>   I do not want it to make him alone. To
>   make him 'different'.

>   KENNEDY
>   It would grieve me to see you go but -
>   perhaps you should leave.

>   YANKO
>   Amy now is home. And she is here.

KENNEDY nods.

>   YANKO
>   But my boy - yes, my boy will leave, when
>   he is a man. I do not want he farm and
>   herd sheep. Not like me.

He looks at Kennedy.

>   YANKO
>   I want him to be like you.

Kennedy is moved. He covers it - as is his way.

>   KENNEDY
>   Like me? I would certainly think twice
>   about that.

>   YANKO
>   Yes! I want him to have the learning of
>   great men. I want him to love the mystery
>   of our universe - yes, like you. You will
>   help him?

Kennedy is so moved it takes him a moment to answer.

>   KENNEDY
>   I would be proud to.

>   YANKO
>   Yes?

>   KENNEDY
>   Yes.

>   YANKO
>   Then all is good.

Kennedy looks at him thoughtfully for a moment.

(CONTINUED)

                         KENNEDY
                You know, it is not healthy to be too
                isolated. You should come to visit me.
                I've missed our conversations - and my
                chess hasn't got any better either.

                         YANKO
                And Amy?

                         KENNEDY
                Amy?

                         YANKO
                Is Amy to visit with me too?

Kennedy is taken aback.

                         KENNEDY
                Well. It wasn't what I had in mind but -
                but yes, I expect that it would be --

                         YANKO
                You do not like Amy.

                         KENNEDY
                Yanko, that's not true.

                         YANKO
                Is true. I have seen your eyes.

                         KENNEDY
                I bear Amy no malice at all. I just don't
                feel that she would make a very good
                companion over dinner.

Yanko nods, sombrely. He turns away.

                         YANKO
                Thank you, Doctor.

Yanko tips his cap and walks away.
                                              AMENDED 3/9/96
                         KENNEDY
                Yanko! What is the matter?

Yanko keeps walking, doesn't turn. Another bout of coughing
takes him - but Kennedy is too upset to notice.

                         KENNEDY
                Yanko!

Kennedy stops, at a loss - then is angered by Yanko's
retreating back.

                                              (CONTINUED)

183 CONTINUED: 183

                    KENNEDY
          Amy cannot make you happy on her own! You
          need --

Kennedy breaks off, suddenly humiliated in front of himself.

Kennedy watches Yanko disappear over the hill.

183A INT. MISS SWAFFER'S BEDROOM. NIGHT. (THE 'PRESENT')   183A

KENNEDY looks haunted as if by the spectre of what is to
come. He speaks as if making a case.

                    KENNEDY
          It was a bad winter. No, he was homesick.   *
          Physiologically, that was the fateful   *
          difference.   *

Miss. Swaffer lies in her bed. She is passionately involved
in the debate - the battle - between them.

                    MISS SWAFFER
          Amy was his home.

Kennedy looks at her.

                    MISS SWAFFER
          He survived the horror of the wreck. He
          learned our tounge. He endured their
          hatred and violence. He earned his
          property and his job. And he did these
          things beacuse he found his home in the
          heart of Amy Foster - as she found her
          home in his.

                    KENNEDY
          She did not take care of him!

Miss Swaffer sees the raging agony in Kennedy's soul; and she
is sad for him.

Kennedy turns away.

                    MISS SWAFFER   *
          Please, sit down.   *

Kennedy takes the chair by the bed. Miss Swaffer knows that *
now, she must heal Kennedy. Gently: *

                    MISS SWAFFER   *
          You cannot imagine how much she took to   *
          care for him.   *

Kennedy looks at her.   *

184   EXT. SWAFFER'S FARM. DAY.   184

The yard is lashed by grey rain. YANKO, carrying a bale of
hay from the barn, drops it as he is seized by a racking
cough. SWAFFER, passing, frowns sagely.

                    SWAFFER
          I was you I'd take that cough on home and   *
          keep warm.

YANKO isn't clear what he means.

                    SWAFFER
          Go home and keep warm!

YANKO shivers and nods.

185   INT. AMY'S COTTAGE - DOWNSTAIRS. EVENING.   185

The room: a wicker cradle on the floor, a kettle spouting
steam on the hob, child's linen drying on the fender. YANKO
lies half-dressed on the couch, drenched in sweat. He murmurs
feverishly, drags off his blankets. He opens his eyes, sees:

Amy wrapping Stefan in a shawl.

Yanko reaches out feeble arms. He mutters in Ukrainian.

                    YANKO
          Miy malen'kiy. Khody do mene.

AMY doesn't understand - but is concerned at Yanko's
condition. She puts Stefan into his crib and hurries over as
YANKO - disoriented by fever - struggles to rise. He waves
his arms and shouts, his eyes momentarily wild and angry.

                    YANKO
          Dai menee mogo khlopchyka.   *

Yanko breaks into a spasm of violent coughing. Amy hauls   *
Yanko back onto the bed and holds him upright until the spasm
passes. A skein of tenacious phlegm clings to his lips and
chin. Amy wipes it away with a handkerchief and settles him
back on the pillows. Throughout Yanko appears unaware of her.
Stefan starts crying in his crib. Amy glances from the crib
to Yanko.

                    AMY
          Please, just stay on the couch. I'm going
          to ask for someone to sit with us, to
          help with Stefan - your little man.
          Please, stay on the couch.

Yanko falls back into a mumbling semi-doze.

                                              (CONTINUED)

185 CONTINUED: 185

        As she speaks Amy wraps herself and the baby in an oilskin.
        She opens the door and looks back at Yanko - semi conscious.
        She steps out into the rain.

185a EXT. KENNEDY'S HOUSE. NIGHT.   185a

        Rain. KENNEDY walks from his house to his carriage and loads
        his bag inside. He turns to the sound of hooves.

        SWAFFER pulls up on his white mare.

                        SWAFFER
                I sent Yanko home this morning. You could
                hear his chest crackling clear across the
                yard. Thought you ought to know.

                        KENNEDY
                I'll pass by the cottage.

        Swaffer gives the fine carriage a dubious look.

                        SWAFFER
                I'd think twice about taking the cart,
                there. The roads're going to get a sight
                worse before the night's out.

        Kennedy climbs up on the seat beneath the carriage's hood.

                        KENNEDY
                I have forty miles to make. But thank you
                for the advice.

        Swaffer watches with steady eyes as Kennedy snaps the reins
        and pulls away.

186 EXT. THE HILLS. EVENING.   186

        AMY struggles against the driving rain towards...

187 ISAAC FOSTER'S COTTAGE.   187

        AMY bangs on the door. It opens. MARY FOSTER answers. She
        stares at AMY coldly. Then a hint of triumph.

                        MARY
                So he's thrown you out at last.

        AMY swallows her pride. She shakes her head.

                        AMY
                My husband is sick. Very sick. I need
                someone to help me sit with him.

        The baby murmurs, hidden in its bundle beneath Amy's coat.
        MARY sees the bundle. Her heart squeezes. She hardens it.

                                                          (CONTINUED)

187 CONTINUED: 187

                    MARY
          You never thought to bring our grandson
          to visit before.

                    AMY
          You never invited us.

                    MARY
          Then ask Old Swaffer. I expect he's
          invited you.

                    AMY
          Swaffer's is six miles. The Smiths' even
          further.

They stare at each other across a great gulf of pain. From
inside the house comes a shout.

                    ISAAC FOSTER
          Mary? This draught'll be the death of us!
          Who's out there?

Mary, her eyes on Amy, calls inside over her shoulder.

                    MARY
          No one! Just a gypsy woman, selling
          curses!

Amy stares at Mary - whose eyes do not soften.

                    AMY
          I always loved you, Mama.

Mary, struck through, cringes inwardly.

                    AMY
          Even if you could never love me.

Amy turns and walks away down the path.

Mary stands watching her from the doorway until --

AMY disappears into the rain.

188 EXT. THE TALFOURD ROAD. NIGHT.   188

AMY walks back up the hill. She hears the rattle of wheels
and hooves and peers up from under her hat.

A CARRIAGE with its yellow lantern approaches.

AMY steps out into the road and waves. THE HORSE is reined
in, squealing. The Carriage judders to a halt. AMY steps
aside. An angry face peers down.

                                              (CONTINUED)

188   CONTINUED: 188

                              DRIVER
                    What the bloody hell? You could've been
                    killed.

The coachman recognizes her, draws back with a grunt. A
woman's head in a bonnet sticks out of the carriage. AMY goes
over: it's MRS. FINN. She sees Amy. Shakes her head in
irritation as if not surprised.

                              MRS. FINN
                    What on earth are you doing out here with
                    that poor infant? Do you want to kill
                    him?

                              AMY
                    Please, ma'am, my husband is taken very
                    poorly. I need someone to help sit with
                    him.

                              MRS. FINN
                    I have my own to look after. As do we
                    all.

Amy blinks in the rain. Mrs. Finn hides behind her bonnet.

                              MRS. FINN
                    You just get that baby indoors. Driver!

The whip cracks. AMY watches the carriage clatter away into
the dark. She starts back towards the cottage.

189   INT. AMY'S COTTAGE. NIGHT.   189

The door opens and AMY enters, drenched. She looks:

YANKO lies mumbling, half-naked on the bed. Amy rushes over,
drags the blanket across him. Then starts to unwrap Stefan.

                                                        CUT TO

190   THE SAME -- LATER.   190

Stefan in his crib. AMY piles logs on the fire.

There's a knock on the door. It opens and Kennedy sticks his
head in from the rain.

                              KENNEDY
                    Amy?

AMY turns - surprised and relieved. Kennedy shrugs off his
oilskins.

                              KENNEDY
                    My God, what a night! There's sickness
                    all over the shop. Old Swaffer asked me
                    to look in on our man.

                                                    (CONTINUED)

190 CONTINUED: 190

                              AMY
                    He keeps on saying something. I don't
                    know what.

          Kennedy pays little attention - he has a lot to do. AMY
          watches him stride briskly over to Yanko with his bag.

191 THE SAME -- LATER.   191

          KENNEDY: sits on the edge of the bed with a stethoscope to
          Yanko's chest. Yanko is unconscious. Kennedy looks concerned
          as he continues his examination.

                              AMY
                    I can't understand what he says.

                              KENNEDY
                    His lungs are congested - he has a
                    pneumonia. A high fever. That's what is
                    making him senseless. Can't you ask
                    someone to come in, just for tonight?

                              AMY
                    Please, sir. Nobody seems to care to
                    come.

          Kennedy shakes his head in shame. He packs his equipment. As
          he shoulders his oil skins back on he instructs her.

                              KENNEDY
                    The fever will get worse before it
                    breaks. It is very important that he
                    receive the greatest care. You may sponge
                    his brow but keep him covered. As much
                    fluid as he will take, and this --

          He takes a bottle of linctus from his bag.

                              KENNEDY
                    It will help the fever a little, and
                    there's a touch of opium to give him some
                    rest. Two tablespoon every six hours.

          He puts the bottle on the table and dons his hat. He sees the
          worry on her face.

                              KENNEDY
                    I must go now. The roads are already dire
                    and I have another fifteen miles to make.

                              AMY
                    Mr. Swaffer might come over, sir, if you
                    were to ask him.

                                                        (CONTINUED)

191   CONTINUED: 191

                         KENNEDY
                Mr Swaffer? I'm afraid my rounds will
                take me in the opposite direction. I
                cannot neglect them.

Amy nods, turns away. Kennedy hesitates, then puts a hand on
her shoulder.

                         KENNEDY
                I will ask while I'm about about if
                anyone else won't come over to help you.

He attempts a reassuring smile and squeezes her shoulder.

He goes and opens the door. Rain gusts in. Amy looks at him.

                         KENNEDY
                And I'll try to pass by again myself
                later on.

Kennedy sees the need in Amy's face. He looks at the clock on
the mantle:

INSERT: the clock face reads a quarter-past-one.

                         KENNEDY
                I'll be back around half-past three.

AMY: grateful. KENNEDY turns away then presses on. AMY looks
at Yanko. She follows Kennedy to the door.

192   EXT. TALFOURD HILL. NIGHT.   192

KENNEDY: leaning into the wind and rain as he walks to his
carriage. As he climbs up he looks back, sees:

AMY standing in the doorway.

KENNEDY waves at her to go inside. Then pulls away.

As Kennedy disappears into the night AMY turns back and
closes the door on the rain-swept cottage.

193   INT. THE COTTAGE - LATER.   193

The baby: asleep in its cradle.

AMY bends over Yanko with a glass of water.

YANKO: his eyes are closed. He mutters incomprehensibly. His
hands reach out and make strange plucking movements in the
air. Amy lifts his head and puts the glass to his lips. Yanko
tosses his head irritably and the water slops down his chest.
Amy puts the glass down and tries to push his arms under the
sheet, but Yanko persists. She looks up.

                                              (CONTINUED)

193   CONTINUED: 193

INSERT: the clock face - it's five past three.

AMY takes the linctus bottle and a spoon from the table and
sits on the bed. She pours a spoonful and tries to get it
into Yanko's mouth. He jerks his head and utters a cry. The
linctus spills down his cheek. The baby starts crying. AMY
whispers in Yanko's ear.

                    AMY
          Please be quiet, my love. My beauty.
          Please. You must take this. Kennedy said
          so. Kennedy.

She pushes his waving arms down and, abandoning the spoon,
tries to put the neck of the bottle to his lips. Yanko gives
out a loud, guttural cry. His arm jerks violently, smashing
into her chest and face. Amy reels back against the table.

The linctus bottle slips from her fingers and SMASHES on the
stone flags of the floor.

AMY looks down at the broken bottle - a moment of horror.
Then she calms herself. Stefan's cries draw her.

She puts the wicker crib on a chair by the bed and sits with
one hand rocking Stefan and the other sponging Yanko's face.

                    AMY
          I'm here, my love. And Stefan - your
          little man. We'll take care of you.

YANKO squirms deliriously - suddenly louder, more restless.
His 'words' are unformed sounds - primitive, feral. A grunt.
A sigh. A gasp. Sudden, sharp cries - whether of pain or fear
or anger it's impossible to say. Amy glances at --

The clock: it's three-fifteen.

                    AMY
          Kennedy is coming. Kennedy.

194   EXT. A REMOTE FARM. NIGHT.   194

A filthy night. The storm rages and howls around the
farmhouse. A carriage stands outside. The door opens and
Kennedy - carrying his bag - battles through the wind towards
his carriage and climbs in.

Kennedy's carriage pulls away.

195   INT. AMY'S COTTAGE. NIGHT.   195

Baby Stefan: sleeping in the cradle at Amy's side.

AMY: watching Yanko -- who is silent, but breathing rapidly.

                                        (CONTINUED)

195   CONTINUED: 195

SUDDENLY: Yanko sits upright, hair plastered to his cheek,
and opens his eyes. He blinks, disoriented. He shouts out.

                    YANKO
          Vody!!

AMY: staring at him. YANKO turns his head, sees her - but his
wild, staring eyes show no trace of recognition.

                    YANKO
          Vody, bud' laska! Kovtok vody!

He waits. AMY doesn't reply. She is very tense. She glances
at the cradle - the sleeping babe.

                    AMY
          Kennedy will be here soon. Doctor
          Kennedy. Just wait for him.

                    YANKO
          Vody!

Amy reaches out and wipes the hair from his face. Yanko
knocks her hand away, his eyes unreadable.

                    YANKO
          Vody!

196   EXT. THE ROAD. NIGHT.   196

As Kennedy's carriage ploughs through the rain he comes upon: *

A WAGON - stranded, it's wheel deep in mud. It is BLOCKING   *
the road. Two farm labourers struggle to lift the wheel free.   *

KENNEDY - urgently - leaps from his carriage and goes over.   *
The wagon's horses are skittish. The labourers' wet faces   *
look up at him - helpless, apologetic.   *

Kennedy looks in the wagon - it's full of milk churns.   *

Kennedy siezes one of the churns.   *

                    KENNEDY   *
          Come on! We must lighten the load!   *

197   INT. AMY AND YANKO'S COTTAGE. NIGHT.   197

YANKO: burning with fever, is amazed that Amy has ignored
him. She stares at him in confusion. He suddenly shouts. He
cannot mean to be - but he is frightening.

                    YANKO
          Vody! Eemenem Boga! Dayte menee vody!

AMY recoils but doesn't leave his side. She tries, gently.

                                                    (CONTINUED)

197 CONTINUED: 197

                         AMY
              Yanko, you must speak English. English. I
              don't know what you want.

In this state Yanko wouldn't understand her even if she spoke
to him in his own language. He starts to plead - to her, to
the ceiling, to no-one knows what.

                         YANKO
              Bud' laska, lyuba, ya vmirayu veed
              spragy. Sklyanka vodu - otse vse, chogo
              ya proshu. Bud' laska. Mama? Chy tse vy,
              mama? Sontse tak peche. Ya tseeliy den'
              pratsyuvav. Proshu, dayte menee trokhy
              vody.

AMY'S FACE: as she listens to him pleading in a stream of
incomprehensible dialect. Tears well into her eyes.

                         AMY
              I don't know what you're saying, my love.
              I don't understand you. Please.

Amy looks at the clock: it's five minutes past four. She goes
to the door, drags it open, looks out and sees:

NOTHING but the raging storm. AMY turns back to Yanko.

                         AMY
              Please. I don't know how to help you. I
              don't know what you want. Speak to me.

YANKO can't understand. Angrily:

                         YANKO
              Chomu ty tse robish zee mnoyu?

AMY: tears roll down her cheeks. Yanko becomes even angrier.

                         YANKO
              Adzhe ya tveey cholovik. Ya ye tvoya
              rodina. Ya vash sin. Kheeba zh ya ne
              pratsyuyu tyazhko? Kheeba zh ya vas ne
              kokhayu? Ya dobriy sin. Dayte menee vody.

Yanko swings his legs from the bed. Amy starts towards him.

                         AMY
              No. You must lie down. Let me give you
              some water.

Amy reaches for an earthenware jug from the table but --

As Yanko tries to stand up his legs give way and he grabs
blindly for the edge of Stefan's crib. The crib starts to
topple. Stefan cries.

                                              (CONTINUED)

Amy lets go of the jug and rushes over -- grabs the crib and
steadies it with one hand. Her other arm she throws around
Yanko's chest and pushes him back onto the bed. As he falls
back, he lashes out blindly. His hand catches Amy across the
face. She ignores it, lets go of the crib, clasps him by the
shoulders.

> AMY
> Don't. Don't, please.

Yanko shrugs her away fiercely, still trying to get up. Amy
takes Stefan from the crib and steps back, away from the bed.

> AMY
> You mustn't harm the baby. I know you
> don't mean to, but you mustn't. I won't
> let you. Just tell me what you want.

YANKO: now very angry.

> YANKO
> Shcho zh ya take zrobiv, shcho ya ne
> mozhu may vody? Day menee vody, zaraz
> zhe! Zaraz zhe, ya skasav!

AMY: fearful, clutching the baby.

> AMY
> Doctor Kennedy will be here. Your friend.

YANKO: a gust of rage sweeps over him. He lurches to his
feet. His legs give out again and he staggers to support
himself on the table. His face is CRAZED with anger. He looks
terrifying. He sees right before him:

The jug of water on the table.

In a spasm of unhinged rage he sweeps the jug from the table.

It shatters on the flags. STILL: Amy holds her ground.

> AMY
> Please, my love. Don't. Don't.

YANKO glares at her from the other side of the table.

> YANKO
> KOVTOK VODY - OTSE VSE, CHOGO YA PROSHU!

AMY, weeping, shakes her head in bewilderment.

YANKO: shouts in a terrible voice.

> YANKO
> ZHEENKO!!

                                                    (CONTINUED)

197 CONTINUED: 197

He lurches around the table, arms reaching out to grab -- the
baby from her arms? Her? She doesn't know what he wants - and
at that moment neither, now, does he. Amy evades him. He
falls to his hands and knees, groping towards her.

AMY snatches her oilskin and runs to the door. She drags it
open. Rain gusts in. She looks back:

YANKO crawls towards her, blinking, dazed.

    AMY
  Kennedy will be here. I must --

YANKO staggers to his feet, his mind gone, lurches forward.

AMY stumbles out of the door into the darkness...

198 EXT. TALFOURD HILL. NIGHT. 198

AMY flees into the stormy night, clutching her baby.

YANKO reels to the door. A thunderbolt crashes. A squall of
rain lashes his face. And for a second his eyes clear - and a
word rises from his fevered brain - a name. He looks out as:

A flash of lightning illuminates AMY as she bursts through
the wicket gate at the foot of the garden.

YANKO's voice rings out terribly behind her.

    YANKO
  AMY!

AMY runs onward into the darkness without turning back.

    YANKO
  AMY FOSTER!

199 EXT. THE MOORS. NIGHT. 199

AMY fights her way across the moors in the banshee rain, the
monstrous night. Clutched under her coat is Stefan.

200 EXT. THE ROAD. NIGHT. 200

KENNEDY and the labourers stack the churns by the road -   *
Kennedy urgently, letting them fall and spill where they *
will. The wagon is now empty. Kennedy motions to the men. *
They all throw their shoulders to the bogged wheel.   *

201 EXT. SWAFFER'S FARM. NIGHT. 201

AMY struggles across the moor in the storm. She seems lost -
she looks this way and that in the darkness. Desperation.
Then she stops as --

(CONTINUED)

201 CONTINUED: 201

A bolt of lightning crackles from the sky and explodes   *
against the trunk of a tall pine tree. As the tree topples,   *
smoking, she sees next to it: TWO more TALL PINES.   *

Amy runs up to the trees in relief. They are Yanko's trees.   *

202 INT. SWAFFER'S FARMHOUSE. NIGHT.   202

Swaffer - in a long nightshirt - opens the door. He is
actually shocked as --

AMY -- half-drowned -- stumbles inside from the rain.

203 THE SAME -- LATER.   203

MISS SWAFFER - nightdress, robe, wheelchair - tenderly
accepts Stefan from Amy's arms. Swaffer - now dressed for the
weather - pokes his head in from outside.

                         SWAFFER
               The mare's ready.

Miss Swaffer reads the anxiety in Amy's face.

                         MISS SWAFFER
               Your babe will be safe. Go to your
               husband.

204 EXT. THE ROADS. DAWN.   204

Amy sits next to Swaffer on the cart as the white mare
gallops at breakneck speed along the storm-ravaged road.

205 EXT. TALFOURD HILL - AMY'S COTTAGE. DAWN.   205

The storm has passed. KENNEDY, looking exhausted, comes down
the road in his carriage. He glances and sees:

THE COTTAGE DOOR hanging OPEN.

KENNEDY rushes to the little wicket gate, eyes on the
cottage. He pushes the gate: it hits something. He looks:

YANKO lies face down, half-naked, his body in a puddle.

                         KENNEDY
               My God, man!

206 INT. THE COTTAGE. DAWN.   206

KENNEDY carries the half-conscious Yanko through the doorway
and across the cold, cheerless room to the bed. He lays him
down. Catches his breath, sees: the fire dead in the grate;
the lamp smoking, the broken jug.

                                                        (CONTINUED)

206 CONTINUED: 206

                         KENNEDY
           AMY?

His voice rings hollow. He looks down.

YANKO opens his eyes -- haunted.

                         YANKO
           Gone! She's gone.

KENNEDY pulls the blankets over Yanko. He puts a hand to
Yanko's pale, clammy, forehead. He feels his pulse.

                         KENNEDY
           I must get my bag. I'll be back in a
           moment.

He starts to rise but Yanko grasps his arm.

                         YANKO
           Where is she?   *

KENNEDY'S FACE: looking down at him without an answer.

                         KENNEDY   *
           I don't know. Please.

Kennedy tries to release himself but Yanko's fingers are
clenched desperately around his wrist.

                         YANKO   *
           What did I do?   *

Kennedy can't answer.   *

                         YANKO
           Did she not love me now anymore?

Kennedy hesitates.

                         KENNEDY
           I don't -- That is I'm sure --

                         YANKO
           I only asked for water! Only for a little
           water!

Kennedy -- stunned. Then the despair on Yanko's face is too
much. As Yanko sags back Kennedy heaves him up --

A POV from the DOORWAY: KENNEDY clasps Yanko to his chest.
Kennedy's head turns. He sees --

The POV is AMY'S -- she stands on the threshold, looking at
YANKO, who lies in Kennedy's arms with his eyes closed,
breathing in shallow gasps.

                                              (CONTINUED)

206 CONTINUED: 206

> KENNEDY lowers Yanko back down, pulls the blanket over him.
> He walks to the doorway. Kennedy looks at Amy coldly.
>
>   KENNEDY
>   Excuse me. I must get my bag.
>
> KENNEDY pushes past her and hurries towards his carriage.
>
> CLOSE ON:
>
> YANKO, his eyes are shut, he is at his last ebb. AMY'S HAND
> caresses his face. YANKO opens his eyes, sees--
>
> AMY'S FACE - looking down at him with tears in her eyes.
>
> YANKO, dying, reaches out a hand.
>
>   YANKO
>   Stefan? My little man?
>
>   AMY
>   He is safe.
>
> Yanko smiles at the thought. He pulls Amy's face towards his
> own. Their eyes melt into each other.
>
>   YANKO
>   I would change nothing. My love - my
>   gold. I would change nothing!
>
>   AMY   *
>   Nor would I.   *
>
> Yanko shudders for his last breath. He uses it to smile.   *
>
>   YANKO   *
>   We are the lucky ones.   *
>
> The light goes out in his eyes. His head falls back.
>
> THE DOORWAY: Swaffer is looking in from outside. He steps
> back as KENNEDY hurries up with his bag. Kennedy sees:
>
> SWAFFER'S FACE. Swaffer turns and walks away.
>
> Kennedy looks inside. He sees:
>
> YANKO DEAD.
>
>   KENNEDY
>   Yanko! Yanko!
>
> Kennedy rushes across the room. AMY watches silently as
> KENNEDY feels Yanko's carotid pulse. Nothing. He closes
> Yanko's eyelids. Kennedy stands up and looks at Amy with a
> mixture of bewilderment and guilt.

(CONTINUED)

206   CONTINUED: 206

                        KENNEDY
                Why did you leave him? Did you not listen
                to a word I said?

AMY runs her fingers through Yanko's long hair. She turns to
look at Kennedy.

                        KENNEDY
                Why did you let him die?

The spear of the hunter strikes through Amy's very soul.

                        KENNEDY
                All he wanted was water! A drink of
                water!

The accusation is terrible and unjust. But Amy - because she
is Amy - looks at Kennedy without blinking. Then - without   *
saying a word - she turns back to Yanko and strokes his face.   *
                                                                    *
Kennedy stares at her with total incomprehension. Then he   *
stumbles towards the door and leaves.

207   EXT. TALFOURD HILL - AMY'S COTTAGE. DAWN.   207

KENNEDY sits on his carriage. He looks at the cottage, then
turns to look out at:

THE SEA: grey, immense, implacable.

                        KENNEDY (V.O.)
                And of that brave adventurer - who had
                crossed an impossible gulf in order to
                love her - Amy Foster utterted not a   *
                word.   *

KENNEDY blinks, composes himself. He snaps the reins at his
horse and pulls away into the grey dawn.

208   INT. MISS SWAFFER'S ROOM. DAWN.   208

Miss Swaffer's bed -- her legs are once again covered by the
tented sheet. MISS SWAFFER - sits up on the pillows. Her
colour has improved, her fever has broken. Her calm grey
eyes are red rimmed, her face damp with tears. She turns to
look - with great pity - at --

KENNEDY -- who sits in a chair by her bed. He looks
completely shattered. He stares down, his head turned.

                        MISS. SWAFFER
                Doctor? Doctor Kennedy?

Kennedy gets to his feet and shambles over to the window.

                                                    (CONTINUED)

                              KENNEDY
                    Now that he is no longer before her eyes
                    - to excite her imagination into a
                    passion of love or fear - his memory
                    seems to have vanished from her brain as
                    a shadow passes from a screen. And I have
                    asked myself: is his image as utterly
                    gone from her mind as his lithe and
                    striding figure is gone from our fields?

Behind him Kennedy hears --

                              MISS SWAFFER
                    How can you say that?

KENNEDY wheels round. He is pierced by -- Miss Swaffer -
looking into him with her strong - tear stained - eyes and
her immense dignity.

                              MISS SWAFFER
                    A man like you.

                              KENNEDY
                    Miss Swaffer --

                              MISS SWAFFER
                    How could you ask such a thing? How could
                    you even think it? Did your own love
                    blind you to hers?

Kennedy is stunned. He can't speak. He turns away and
gathers his things.

                              MISS SWAFFER
                    Did you not have your own family once,
                    Docter Kennedy?

                              KENNEDY
                    It was many lifetimes ago, Miss Swaffer.

He closes his bag, picks it up, turns to the door.

                              MISS SWAFFER
                    So you have wiped your own shadows from
                    the screen.

Kennedy turns away - as a great surge of grief shakes him to
his core. But he holds his dignity together - as is his way.
He blinks, looks through the window up at --

The two tall pine trees on the hill and the lightning-
bleached skelton of the third.

                              MISS SWAFFER
                    Yanko found his true love.

(CONTINUED)

208   CONTINUED: 208

                        KENNEDY
                 No. His true gold.

Kennedy composes himself, turns.

                        KENNEDY
                 Thank you, Miss Swaffer. For our --
                 conversation.

He goes to the door, opens it. Pauses, as --

                        MISS SWAFFER
                 You carry more - for all of us - than any
                 one man should, James Kennedy. But - you
                 will take care for them, won't you?

Kennedy looks back at her.

209   EXT. TALFOURD HILL. DAY.   209

The rolling hills in bright sunshine.

THE COTTAGE: AMY trims the rose vine on the door trellis.
Around her neck are: Yanko's AMULETS.

                        KENNEDY
                 Hello, Amy.

It's -- KENNEDY. Exhausted. Drained. He draws himself up.

                        KENNEDY
                 Amy - I have wronged you. Grievously. And
                 I have no excuse.

Amy looks at him - into him.

                        KENNEDY
                 Will you forgive me?

Amy walks up to him. Her eyes are full.

                        AMY
                 Who will forgive me?

                        KENNEDY
                 I do.

Amy falls against his chest.

And she cries. In great racking sobs, she cries.

Kennedy puts his arms around her.

                        KENNEDY
                 I do. As did he.

(CONTINUED)

209   CONTINUED: 209

                          AMY
                 I will love him until the end of the   *
                 world.   *

Kennedy deeply moved, looks over her shoulder and sees: *

The boy Stefan - RUNNNING. Kennedy - in spite of all -
smiles. Amy looks at Kennedy -- sees his smile.

The stirring mountain music of Yanko's homeland arises.

And AMY smiles too.

210   INT. THE CAVE. DAY.   210

The music grows - rises - Stefan runs across the great
flickering ochre cavern and -- into the tunnel.

211   EXT. THE BEACH. DAY.   211

Stefan bursts from the tunnel, stops dead on the beach. He
takes a few steps and stares - fascinated - at:

THE POUNDING SEA.

AMY walks from the cave and stands by Stefan on the beach.
Their hair flies in the wind.

Pulling BACK from the beach -- and back --

                       KENNEDY (V.O.)
                 Looking at her now I see wherein he found
                 the truest of true gold.

Further back -- and further --

                       KENNEDY (V.O.)
                 And in the boy - with his wild eyes and
                 shining hair - I seem, always, to see
                 once again the other. The father --

Until -- it is KENNEDY - wind-blown and standing tall - who
watches them from the cliff.

                       KENNEDY (V.O.)
                 -- who was cast out by the mysterious sea
                 to perish - and yet be reborn - in the
                 deeper mystery of passion and despair...

The mountain music approaches a shattering crescendo. We see:
AMY and STEFAN -- and Stefan is DANCING, like his father.
They form double silhouette of gold carved against the hazy,
glittering immensity of -- THE SEA.

                          THE END

STILLS

Above: Yanko *(Vincent Perez)* and Amy *(Rachel Weisz)* walk out in Colebrook Village.

AMY FOSTER
Rachel Weisz

YANKO GOORAL
Vincent Perez

DR. JAMES KENNEDY
Ian McKellen

116

MISS SWAFFER
Kathy Bates

117

Above: Yanko Gooral *(Perez)* and Stefan *(Paul Whitby)* wave farewell to their families in the Ukraine.

Below: A behind-the-scenes shot of the ship carrying Yanko to America being pounded by a storm.

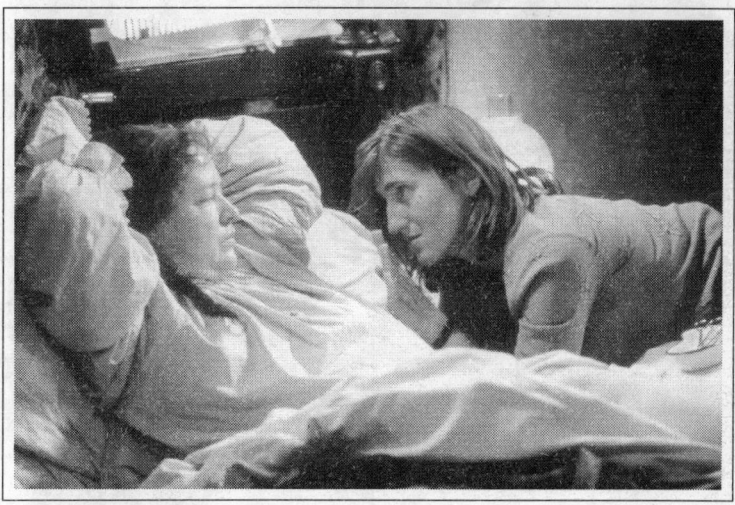

Above: Dr. Kennedy *(Ian McKellen)* making his rounds.
Below: Director Beeban Kidron directs Kathy Bates in her role as Miss Swaffer.

Opposite top: Amy *(Weisz)* visits her family, the Fosters, Isaac *(Tom Bell)* and Mary *(Zoë Wanamaker).*

Opposite bottom: Amy *(Weisz)* on her wedding day wears the green satin ribbon from Yanko.

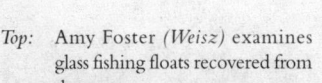

Top: Amy Foster *(Weisz)* examines glass fishing floats recovered from the sea.

Bottom: Yanko *(Perez)* leans against a rock in Amy's cave.

Above: Yanko *(Perez)* invites Amy to dance in the secret and fantastic world of her cave.
Below: Amy *(Weisz)* displays one of her treasures in the cave—a length of yellow chiffon.

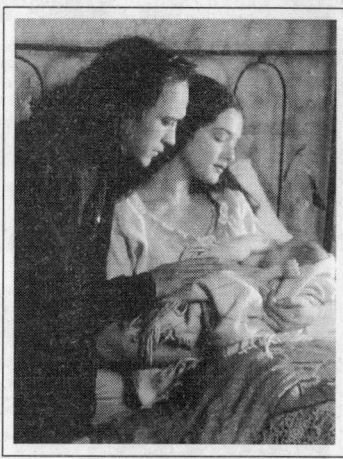

Above: Miss Swaffer *(Kathy Bates)* anticipates the arrival of Amy and Yanko outside the cottage.
Below left: Amy *(Weisz)* and Yanko *(Perez)* make a special visit to Dr. Kennedy's consulting room
to confirm she is with child.
Below right: Yanko *(Perez)* and Amy *(Weisz)*, at home in their cottage, cherish their newborn
son.

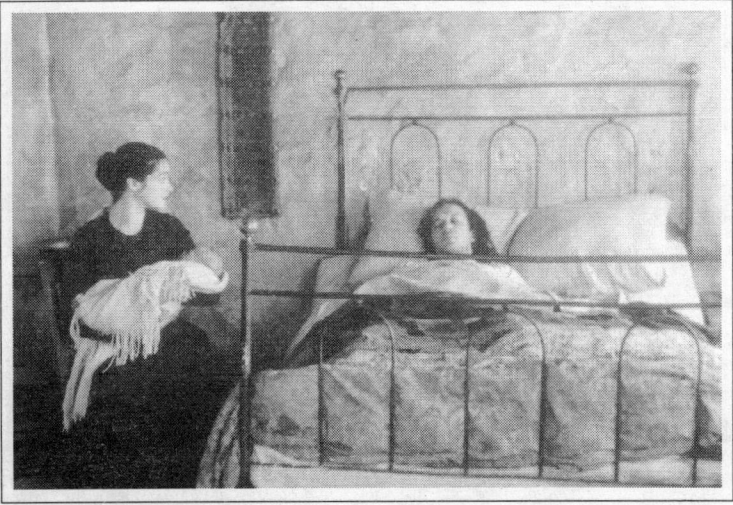

Above: Yanko *(Perez)* proudly holds his swaddled baby.
Below: Amy *(Weisz)* cradles their son while watching over her feverish husband.

Above: Dr. Kennedy *(McKellen)*—anguished—after quarreling with Yanko outside of the cottage.
Below: Amy *(Weisz)*, haunted by the memory of Yanko, shows her son the sea.

AMY FOSTER

BY JOSEPH CONRAD

Kennedy is a country doctor, and lives in Colebrook, on the shores of Eastbay. The high ground rising abruptly behind the red roofs of the little town crowds the quaint High Street against the wall which defends it from the sea. Beyond the seawall there curves for miles in a vast and regular sweep the barren beach of shingle, with the village of Brenzett standing out darkly across the water, a spire in a clump of trees; and still further out the perpendicular column of a lighthouse, looking in the distance no bigger than a lead-pencil, marks the vanishing-point of the land. The country at the back of Brenzett is low and flat; but the bay is fairly well sheltered from the seas, and occasionally a big ship, windbound or through stress of weather, makes use of the anchoring ground a mile and a half due north from you as you stand at the back door of the "Ship Inn" in Brenzett. A dilapidated windmill near by, lifting its shattered arms from a mound no loftier than a rubbish-heap, and a Martello tower squatting at the water's edge half a mile to the south of the Coastguard cottages, are familiar to the skippers of small craft. These are the official seamarks for the patch of trustworthy bottom represented on the Admiralty charts by an irregular oval of dots enclosing several figures six, with a tiny anchor engraved among them, and the legend "mud and shells" over all.

The brow of the upland overtops the square tower of the Colebrook Church The slope is green and looped by a white road. Ascending along this road, you open a valley broad and shallow, a wide green trough of pastures and hedges merging inland into a vista of purple tints and flowing lines closing the view.

In this valley down to Brenzett and Colebrook and up to Darnford, the market town fourteen miles away, lies the practice of my friend Kennedy. He had begun life as surgeon in the Navy, and afterwards had been the companion of a famous traveller, in the days when there were continents with unexplored interiors. His papers on the fauna and flora made him known to scientific societies. And now he had come to a country practice—from choice. The penetrating power of his mind, acting like a corrosive fluid, had destroyed his ambition, I fancy. His intelligence is of a scientific order, of an investigating habit, and of that unappeasable curiosity which believes that there is a particle of a general truth in every mystery.

A good many years ago now, on my return from abroad, he invited me to stay with him. I came readily enough, and as he could not neglect his patients to keep me company, he took me on his rounds—thirty miles or so of an afternoon, sometimes. I waited for him on the roads; the horse reached after the leafy twigs, and, sitting high in the dogcart, I could hear Kennedy's laugh through the half-open door of some cottage. He had a big, hearty laugh that would have fitted a man twice his size, a brisk manner, a bronzed face, and a pair of gray, profoundly attentive eyes. He had the talent of making people talk to him freely, and an inexhaustible patience in listening to their tales.

One day, as we trotted out of a large village into a shady bit of road, I saw on our left hand a low, black cottage, with diamond panes in the windows, a creeper on the end wall, a roof of shingle, and some roses climbing on the rickety trellis-work of the tiny porch. Kennedy pulled up to a walk. A woman, in full sunlight, was throwing a dripping blanket over a line stretched between two old apple-trees. And as the bobtailed, long-necked chestnut, trying to get his head, jerked the left hand, covered by a thick dogskin glove, the doctor raised his voice over the hedge: "How's your child, Amy?"

I had the time to see her dull face, red, not with a mantling blush, but as if her flat cheeks had been vigorously slapped, and to take in the squat figure, the scanty, dusty brown hair drawn into a tight knot at the back of the head. She looked quite young. With a distinct catch in her breath, her voice sounded low and timid.

"He's well, thank you."

We trotted again. "A young patient of yours," I said; and the doctor, flicking the chestnut absently, muttered, "Her husband used to be."

"She seems a dull creature," I remarked, listlessly.

"Precisely," said Kennedy. "She is very passive. It's enough to look at the red hands hanging at the end of those short arms, at those slow, prominent brown eyes, to know the inertness of her mind—an inertness that one would think made it everlastingly safe from all the surprises of imagination. And yet which of us is safe? At any rate, such as you see her, she had enough imagination to fall in love. She's the daughter of one Isaac Foster, who from a small farmer has sunk into a shepherd; the beginning of his misfortunes dating from his run-away marriage with the cook of his widowed father—a well-to-do, apoplectic grazier, who passionately struck his name off his will, and had been heard to utter threats against his life. But this old affair, scandalous enough to serve as a motive for a Greek tragedy, arose from the similarity of their characters. There are other tragedies, less scandalous and of a subtler poignancy, arising from irreconcilable differences and from that fear of the Incomprehensible that hangs over all our heads—over all our heads. . . ."

The tired chestnut dropped into a walk; and the rim of the sun, all red in a speckless sky, touched familiarly the smooth top of a ploughed rise near the road as I had seen it times innumerable touch the distant horizon of the sea. The uniform brownness of the harrowed field glowed with a rose tinge, as though the powdered clods had sweated out in minute pearls of blood the toil of uncounted ploughmen. From the edge of a copse a waggon with two horses was rolling gently along the ridge. Raised above our heads upon the sky-line, it loomed up against the red sun, triumphantly big, enormous, like a chariot of giants drawn by two slow-stepping steeds of legendary pro-portions. And the clumsy figure of the man plodding at the head of the leading horse projected itself on the background of the Infinite with a heroic uncouthness. The end of his carter's whip quivered high up in the blue. Kennedy discoursed.

"She's the eldest of a large family. At the age of fifteen they put her out to service at the New Barns Farm. I attended Mrs. Smith, the tenant's wife, and saw that girl there for the first time. Mrs. Smith, a genteel person with a sharp nose, made her put on a black dress every afternoon. I don't know what induced me to notice her at all. There are faces that call your attention by a curious want of definiteness in their whole aspect, as, walking in a mist, you peer attentively at a vague shape which, after all, may be nothing more curious or strange than a signpost. The only peculiarity I perceived in her was a slight hesitation in her utterance, a sort of preliminary stammer which passes away with the first word. When sharply spoken to, she was apt to lose her head at once; but her heart was of the kindest. She had never been heard to express a dislike for a single human being, and she was tender to every living creature. She was devoted to Mrs. Smith, to Mr. Smith, to their dogs, cats, canaries; and as to Mrs. Smith's gray parrot, its peculiarities exer-cised upon her a positive fascination. Nevertheless, when that outlandish bird, attacked by the cat, shrieked for help in human accents, she ran out into the yard stopping her ears, and did not prevent the crime. For Mrs. Smith this was another evidence of her stupidity; on the other hand, her want of charm, in view of Smith's well-known frivolousness, was a great recommendation. Her shortsighted eyes would swim with pity for a poor mouse in a trap, and she had been seen once by some boys on her knees in the wet grass helping a toad in difficulties. If it's true, as some German fellow has said, that without phosphorus there is no thought, it is still more true that there is no kindness of heart without a certain amount of imagination. She had some. She had even more than is necessary to understand suffering and to be moved by pity. She fell in love under circumstances that leave no room for doubt in the matter; for you need imagination to form a notion of beauty at all, and still more to discover your ideal in an unfamiliar shape.

"How this aptitude came to her, what it did feed upon, is an inscrutable mystery. She was born in the village, and had never been further away from it than Colebrook or perhaps Darnford. She lived for four years with the Smiths. New Barns is an isolated farm-house a mile away from the road, and she was content to look day after day at the same fields, hollows, rises; at the trees and the hedgerows; at the faces of the four men about the farm, always the same—day after day, month after month, year after year. She never showed a desire for conversation, and, as it seemed to me, she did not know how to smile. Sometimes of a fine Sunday afternoon she would put on her best dress, a pair of stout boots, a large gray hat trimmed with a black feather (I've seen her in that finery), seize an absurdly slender parasol, climb over two stiles, tramp over three fields and along two hundred yards of road—never further. There stood Foster's cottage. She would help her mother to give their tea to the younger children, wash up the crockery, kiss the little ones, and go back to the farm. That was all. All the rest, all the change, all the relaxation. She never seemed to wish for anything more. And then she fell in love. She fell in love silently, obstinately—perhaps helplessly. It came slowly, but when it came it worked like a powerful spell; it was love as the Ancients understood it: an irresistible and fateful impulse—a possession! Yes, it was in her to become haunted and possessed by a face, by a presence, fatally, as though she had been a pagan worshipper of form under a joyous sky—and to be awakened at last from that mysterious forgetfulness of self, from that enchantment, from that transport, by a fear resembling the unaccountable terror of a brute. . . ."

With the sun hanging low on its western limit, the expanse of the grasslands framed in the counter-scarps of the rising ground took on a gorgeous and sombre aspect. A sense of penetrating sadness, like that inspired by a grave strain of music, disengaged itself from the silence of the fields. The men we met walked past, slow, unsmiling, with downcast eyes, as if the melancholy of an over-burdened earth had weighted their feet, bowed their shoulders, borne down their glances.

"Yes," said the doctor to my remark, "one would think the earth is under a curse, since of all her children these that cling to her the closest are uncouth in body and as leaden of gait as if their very hearts were loaded with chains. But here on this same road you might have seen amongst these heavy men a being lithe, supple and long-limbed, straight like a pine, with something striving upwards in his appearance as though the heart within him had been buoyant. Perhaps it was only the force of the contrast, but when he was passing one of these villagers here, the soles of his feet did not seem to me to touch the dust of the road. He vaulted over the stiles, paced these slopes with a long elastic stride that made him noticeable at a great distance, and had lustrous black eyes. He was so different from the mankind around that, with his freedom of movement, his soft—a little startled, glance, his olive complexion and graceful bearing, his humanity suggested to me the nature of a woodland creature. He came from there."

The doctor pointed with his whip, and from the summit of the descent seen over the rolling tops of the trees in a park by the side of the road, appeared the level sea far below us, like the floor of an immense edifice inlaid with bands of dark ripple, with still trails of glitter, ending in a belt of glassy water at the foot of the sky. The light blur of smoke, from an invisible steamer, faded on the great clearness of the horizon like the mist of a breath on a mirror; and, inshore, the white sails of a coaster, with the appearance of disentangling themselves slowly from under the branches, floated clear of the foliage of the trees.

"Shipwrecked in the bay?" I said.

"Yes; he was a castaway. A poor emigrant from Central Europe bound to America and washed ashore here in a storm. And for him, who knew nothing of the earth, England was an undiscovered country. It was some time before he learned its name; and for all I know he might have expected to find wild beasts or wild men here, when, crawling in the dark over the sea-wall, he rolled down the other side into a dyke, where it was another miracle he didn't get drowned. But he struggled instinctively like an animal under a net, and this blind struggle threw him out into a field. He must have been, indeed, of a tougher fibre than he looked to withstand without expiring such buffetings, the violence of his exertions, and so much fear. Later on, in his broken English that resembled curiously the speech of a young child, he told me himself that he put his trust in God, believing he was no longer in this world. And truly—he would add—how was he to know? He fought his way against the rain and the gale on all fours, and crawled at last among some sheep huddled close under the lee of a hedge. They ran off in all directions, bleating in the darkness, and he welcomed the first familiar sound he heard on these shores. It must have been two in the morning then. And this is all we know of the manner of his landing, though he did not arrive unattended by any means. Only his grisly company did not begin to come ashore till much later in the day. . . ."

The doctor gathered the reins, clicked his tongue; we trotted down the hill. Then turning, almost directly, a sharp corner into High Street, we rattled over the stones and were home.

Late in the evening Kennedy, breaking a spell of moodiness that had come over him, returned to the story. Smoking his pipe, he paced the long room from end to end. A reading-lamp concentrated all its light upon the papers on his desk; and, sitting by the open window, I saw, after the windless, scorching day, the frigid splendour of a hazy sea lying motionless under the moon. Not a whisper, not a splash, not a stir of the shingle, not a footstep, not a sigh came up from the earth below—never a sign of life but the scent of climbing jasmine: and Kennedy's voice, speaking behind me, passed through the wide casement, to vanish outside in a chill and sumptuous stillness.

". . . . The relations of shipwrecks in the olden time tell us of much suffering. Often the castaways were only saved from drowning to die miserably from starvation on a barren coast; others suffered violent death or else slavery, passing through years of precarious existence with people to whom their strangeness was an object of suspicion, dislike or fear. We read about these things, and they are very pitiful. It is indeed hard upon a man to find himself a lost stranger, helpless, incomprehensible, and of a mysterious origin, in some obscure corner of the earth. Yet amongst all the adventurers shipwrecked in all the wild parts of the world, there is not one, it seems to me, that ever had to suffer a fate so simply tragic as the man I am speaking of, the most innocent of adventurers cast out, by the sea in the bight of this bay, almost within sight from this very window.

"He did not know the name of his ship. Indeed, in the course of time we discovered he did not even know that ships had names—'like Christian people'; and when, one day, from the top of Talfourd Hill, he beheld the sea lying open to his view, his eyes roamed afar, lost in an air of wild surprise, as though he had never seen such a sight before. And probably he had not. As far as I could make out, he had been hustled together with many others on board an emigrant ship at the mouth of the Elbe, too bewildered to take note of his surroundings, too weary to see anything, too anxious to care. They were driven below into the 'tween-deck and battened down from the very start. It was a low timber dwelling—he would say—with wooden beams overhead, like the houses in his country, but you went into it down a ladder. It was very large, very cold, damp and sombre, with places in the manner of wooden boxes where people had to sleep one above another, and it kept on rocking all ways at once all the time. He crept into one of these boxes and lay down there in the clothes in which he had left his home many days before, keeping his bundle and his stick by his side. People groaned, children cried, water dripped, the lights went out, the walls of the place creaked, and everything was being shaken so that in one's little box one dared not lift one's head. He had lost touch with his only companion (a young man from the same valley, he said), and all the time a great noise of wind went on outside and heavy blows fell—boom! boom! An awful sickness overcame him, even to the point of making him neglect his prayers. Besides, one could not tell whether it was morning or evening. It seemed always to be night in that place.

"Before that he had been travelling a long, long time on the iron track. He looked out of the window, which had a wonderfully clear glass in it, and the trees, the houses, the fields, and the long roads seemed to fly round and round about him till his head swam. He gave me to understand that he had on his passage beheld uncounted multitudes of people—whole nations—all dressed in such clothes as the rich wear. Once he was made to get out of the carriage, and slept through a night on a bench in a house of bricks with his bundle under his head; and once for many hours he had to sit on a floor of flat stones, dozing, with his knees up and with his bundle between his feet. There was a roof over him, which seemed made of glass, and was so high that the tallest mountain-pine he had ever seen would have had room to grow under it. Steam-machines rolled in at one end and out at the other. People swarmed more than you can see on a feast-day round the miraculous Holy Image in the yard of the Carmelite Convent down in the plains where, before he left his home, he drove his mother in a wooden cart:—a pious old woman who wanted to offer prayers and make a vow for his safety. He could not give me an idea of how large and lofty and full of noise and smoke and gloom, and clang of iron, the place was, but someone had told him it was called

Berlin. Then they rang a bell, and another steam-machine came in, and again he was taken on and on through a land that wearied his eyes by its flatness without a single bit of a hill to be seen anywhere. One more night he spent shut up in a building like a good stable with a litter of straw on the floor, guarding his bundle amongst a lot of men, of whom not one could understand a single word he said. In the morning they were all led down to the stony shores of an extremely broad muddy river, flowing not between hills but between houses that seemed immense. There was a steam-machine that went on the water, and they all stood upon it packed tight, only now there were with them many women and children who made much noise. A cold rain fell, the wind blew in his face; he was wet through, and his teeth chattered. He and the young man from the same valley took each other by the hand.

"They thought they were being taken to America straight away, but suddenly the steam-machine bumped against the side of a thing like a great house on the water. The walls were smooth and black, and there uprose, growing from the roof as it were, bare trees in the shape of crosses, extremely high. That's how it appeared to him then, for he had never seen a ship before. This was the ship that was going to swim all the way to America. Voices shouted, everything swayed; there was a ladder dipping up and down. He went up on his hands and knees in mortal fear of falling into the water below, which made a great splashing. He got separated from his companion, and when he descended into the bottom of that ship his heart seemed to melt suddenly within him.

"It was then also, as he told me, that he lost contact for good and all with one of those three men who the summer before had been going about through all the little towns in the foothills of his country. They would arrive on market-days driving in a peasant's cart, and would set up an office in an inn or some other Jew's house. There were three of them, of whom one with a long beard looked venerable; and they had red cloth collars round their necks and gold lace on their sleeves like Government officials. They sat proudly behind a long table; and in the next room, so that the common people shouldn't hear, they kept a cunning telegraph machine, through which they could talk to the Emperor of America. The fathers hung about the door, but the young men of the mountains would crowd up to the table asking many questions, for there was work to be got all the year round at three dollars a day in America, and no military service to do.

"But the American Kaiser would not take everybody. Oh, no! He himself had a great difficulty in getting accepted, and the venerable man in uniform

133

had to go out of the room several times to work the telegraph on his behalf. The American Kaiser engaged him at last at three dollars, he being young and strong. However, many able young men backed out, afraid of the great distance; besides, those only who had some money could be taken. There were some who sold their huts and their land because it cost a lot of money to get to America; but then, once there, you had three dollars a day, and if you were clever you could find places where true gold could be picked up on the ground. His father's house was getting over full. Two of his brothers were married and had children. He promised to send money home from America by post twice a year. His father sold an old cow, a pair of piebald mountain ponies of his own raising, and a cleared plot of fair pasture land on the sunny slope of a pine-clad pass to a Jew innkeeper, in order to pay the people of the ship that took men to America to get rich in a short time.

"He must have been a real adventurer at heart, for how many of the greatest enterprises in the conquest of the earth had for their beginning just such a bargaining away of the paternal cow for the mirage or true gold far away! I have been telling you more or less in my own words what I learned fragmentarily in the course of two or three years, during which I seldom missed an opportunity of a friendly chat with him. He told me this story of his adventure with many flashes of white teeth and lively glances of black eyes, at first in a sort of anxious baby-talk, then, as he acquired the language, with great fluency, but always with that singing, soft, and at the same time vibrating intonation that instilled a strangely penetrating power into the sound of the most familiar English words, as if they had been the words of an unearthly language. And he always would come to an end, with many emphatic shakes of his head, upon that awful sensation of his heart melting within him directly he set foot on board that ship. Afterwards there seemed to come for him a period of blank ignorance, at any rate as to facts. No doubt he must have been abominably seasick and abominably unhappy—this soft and passionate adventurer, taken thus out of his knowledge, and feeling bitterly as he lay in his emigrant bunk his utter loneliness; for his was a highly sensitive nature. The next thing we know of him for certain is that he had been hiding in Hammond's pigpound by the side of the road to Norton, six miles, as the crow flies, from the sea. Of these experiences he was unwilling to speak: they seemed to have seared into his soul a sombre sort of wonder and indignation. Through the rumours of the country-side, which lasted for a good many days after his arrival, we know that the fishermen of West Colebrook had been disturbed and startled by heavy knocks against the walls of weatherboard cottages, and by a voice crying piercingly strange words in the night. Several of them turned out even, but, no doubt, he had fled in sudden alarm at their rough angry tones hailing each other in the darkness. A sort of frenzy must have helped him up the steep Norton hill. It was he, no doubt, who early the following morning had been seen lying (in a swoon, I should say) on the roadside grass by the Brenzett carrier, who actually got down to have a nearer look, but drew back, intimidated by the perfect immobility, and by something queer in the aspect of that tramp, sleeping so still under the showers. As the day advanced, some children came dashing into school at Norton in such a fright that the schoolmistress went out and spoke indignantly to a 'horrid-looking man' on the road. He edged away, hanging his head, for a few steps, and then suddenly ran off with extraordinary fleetness. The driver of Mr. Bradley's milk-cart made no secret of it that he had lashed with his whip at a hairy sort of gipsy fellow who, jumping up at a turn of the road by the Vents, made a snatch at the pony's bridle. And he caught him a good one, too, right over the face, he said, that made him drop down in the mud a jolly sight quicker than he had jumped up; but it was a good half a mile before he could stop the pony. Maybe that in his desperate endeavours to get help, and in his need to get in touch with someone, the poor devil had tried to stop the cart. Also three boys confessed afterwards to throwing stones at a funny tramp, knocking about all wet and muddy, and, it seemed, very drunk, in the narrow deep lane by the limekilns. All this was the talk of three villages for days; but we have Mrs. Finn's (the wife of Smith's waggoner) unimpeachable testimony that she saw him get over the low wall of Hammond's pig-pound and lurch straight at her, babbling aloud in a voice that was enough to make one die of fright. Having the baby with her in a perambulator, Mrs. Finn called out to him to go away, and as he persisted in coming nearer, she hit him courageously with her umbrella over the head, and, without once looking back, ran like the wind with the perambulator as far as the first house in the village. She stopped then, out of breath, and spoke to old Lewis, hammering there at a heap of stones; and the old chap, taking off his immense black wire goggles, got up on his shaky legs to look where she pointed. Together they followed with their eyes the figure of the man running over a field; they saw him fall down, pick himself up, and run on again, staggering and waving his long arms above his head, in the direction of the New Barns Farm. From that moment he is plainly in the toils of his obscure and touching destiny. There is no doubt after this of what happened to him. All is certain now: Mrs. Smith's intense terror; Amy Foster's stolid conviction held against the other's nervous attack, that the man

135

'meant no harm'; Smith's exasperation (on his return from Darnford Market) at finding the dog barking himself into a fit, the back-door locked, his wife in hysterics; and all for an unfortunate dirty tramp, supposed to be even then lurking in his stackyard. Was he? He would teach him to frighten women.

"Smith is notoriously hot-tempered, but the sight of some nondescript and miry creature sitting cross-legged amongst a lot of loose straw, and swinging itself to and fro like a bear in a cage, made him pause. Then this tramp stood up silently before him, one mass of mud and filth from head to foot. Smith, alone amongst his stacks with this apparition, in the stormy twilight ringing with the infuriated barking of the dog, felt the dread of an inexplicable strangeness. But when that being, parting with his black hands the long matted locks that hung before his face, as you part the two halves of a curtain, looked out at him with glistening, wild, black-and-white eyes, the weirdness of this silent encounter fairly staggered him. He has admitted since (for the story has been a legitimate subject of conversation about here for years) that he made more than one step backwards. Then a sudden burst of rapid, senseless speech persuaded him at once that he had to do with an escaped lunatic. In fact, that impression never wore off completely. Smith has not in his heart given up his secret conviction of the man's essential insanity to this very day.

"As the creature approached him, jabbering in a most discomposing manner, Smith (unaware that he was being addressed as 'gracious lord,' and adjured in God's name to afford food and shelter) kept on speaking firmly but gently to it, and retreating all the time into the other yard. At last, watching his chance, by a sudden charge he bundled him headlong into the wood-lodge, and instantly shot the bolt. Thereupon he wiped his brow, though the day was cold. He had done his duty to the community by shutting up a wandering and probably dangerous maniac. Smith isn't a hard man at all, but he had room in his brain only for that one idea of lunacy. He was not imaginative enough to ask himself whether the man might not be perishing with cold and hunger. Meantime, at first, the maniac made a great deal of noise in the lodge. Mrs. Smith was screaming upstairs, where she had locked herself in her bedroom; but Amy Foster sobbed piteously at the kitchen-door, wringing her hands and muttering, 'Don't! don't!' I daresay Smith had a rough time of it that evening with one noise and another, and this insane, disturbing voice crying obstinately through the door only added to his irritation. He couldn't possibly have connected this troublesome lunatic with the sinking of a ship in Eastbay, of which there had been a rumour in the Darnford market place. And I daresay the man inside had been very near to insanity on that night. Before his excitement collapsed and he became unconscious he was throwing himself violently about in the dark, rolling on some dirty sacks, and biting his fists with rage, cold, hunger, amazement, and despair.

"He was a mountaineer of the eastern range of the Carpathians, and the vessel sunk the night before in Eastbay was the Hamburg emigrant-ship *Herzogin Sophia-Dorothea,* of appalling memory.

"A few months later we could read in the papers the accounts of the bogus 'Emigration Agencies' among the Sclavonian peasantry in the more remote provinces of Austria. The object of these scoundrels was to get hold of the poor ignorant people's homesteads, and they were in league with the local usurers. They exported their victims through Hamburg mostly. As to the ship, I had watched her out of this very window, reaching close-hauled under short canvas into the bay on a dark, threatening afternoon. She came to an anchor, correctly by the chart, off the Brenzett Coastguard station. I remember before the night fell looking out again at the outlines of her spars and rigging that stood out dark and pointed on a background of ragged, slaty clouds like another and a slighter spire to the left of the Brenzett church-tower. In the evening the wind rose. At midnight I could hear in my bed the terrific gusts and the sounds of a driving deluge.

"About that time the Coastguardmen thought they saw the lights of a steamer over the anchoring-ground. In a moment they vanished; but it is clear that another vessel of some sort had tried for shelter in the bay on that awful, blind night, had rammed the German ship amidships (a breach—as one of the divers told me afterwards—'that you could sail a Thames barge through'), and then had gone out either scathless or damaged, who shall say; but had gone out, unknown, unseen, and fatal, to perish mysteriously at sea. Of her nothing ever came to light, and yet the hue and cry that was raised all over the world would have found her out if she had been in existence anywhere on the face of the waters.

"A completeness without a clue, and a stealthy silence as of a neatly executed crime, characterize this murderous disaster, which, as you may remember, had its gruesome celebrity. The wind would have prevented the loudest outcries from reaching the shore; there had been evidently no time for signals of distress. It was death without any sort of fuss. The Hamburg ship, filling all at once, capsized as she sank, and at daylight there was not even the end of a spar to be seen above water. She was missed, of course, and at first the Coastguardmen surmised that she had either dragged her anchor or parted her cable some time during the night, and had been blown out to sea. Then, after the tide turned, the wreck must have shifted a little and released some of the bodies, because a child—a little fair-haired child in a red frock—came ashore abreast of the Martello tower. By the afternoon you could see along three miles of beach dark figures with bare legs dashing in and out of the tumbling foam, and rough-looking men, women with hard faces, children, mostly fair-haired, were being carried, stiff and dripping, on stretchers, on wattles, on ladders, in a long procession past the door of the 'Ship Inn,' to be laid out in a row under the north wall of the Brenzett Church.

"Officially, the body of the little girl in the red frock is the first thing that came ashore from that ship. But I have patients amongst the seafaring population of West Colebrook, and, unofficially, I am informed that very early that morning two brothers, who went down to look after their cobble hauled up on the beach, found a good way from Brenzett, an ordinary ship's hencoop, lying high and dry on the shore, with eleven drowned ducks inside. Their families ate the birds, and the hen-coop was split into firewood with a hatchet. It is possible that a man (supposing he happened to be on deck at the time of the accident) might have floated ashore on that hencoop. He might. I admit it is improbable, but there was the man—and for days, nay, for weeks—it didn't enter our heads that we had amongst us the only living soul that had escaped from that disaster. The man himself, even when he learned to speak intelligibly, could tell us very little. He remembered he had felt better (after the ship had anchored, I suppose), and that the darkness, the wind, and the rain took his breath away. This looks as if he had been on deck some time during that night. But we mustn't forget he had been taken out of his knowledge, that he had been sea-sick and battened down below for four days, that he had no general notion of a ship or of the sea, and therefore could have no definite idea of what was happening to him. The rain, the wind, the darkness he knew; he understood the bleating of the sheep, and he remembered the pain of his wretchedness and misery, his heartbroken astonishment that it was neither seen nor understood, his dismay at finding all the men angry and all the women fierce. He had approached them as a beggar, it is true, he said; but in his country, even if they gave nothing, they spoke gently to beggars. The children in his country were not taught to throw stones at those who asked for compassion. Smith's strategy overcame him completely. The wood-lodge presented the horrible aspect of a dungeon. What would be done to him next? . . . No wonder that Amy Foster appeared to his eyes with the aureole of an angel of light. The girl had not been able to sleep for thinking of the poor man, and in the morning, before the Smiths were up, she slipped out across the back yard. Holding the door of the wood-lodge ajar, she looked in and extended to him half a loaf of white bread—'such bread as the rich eat in my country,' he used to say.

"At this he got up slowly from amongst all sorts of rubbish, stiff, hungry, trembling, miserable, and doubtful. 'Can you eat this?' she asked in her soft and timid voice. He must have taken her for a 'gracious lady.' He devoured ferociously, and tears were falling on the crust. Suddenly he dropped the bread, seized her wrist, and imprinted a kiss on her hand. She was not frightened. Through his forlorn condition she had observed that he was good-looking. She shut the door and walked back slowly to the kitchen. Much later on, she told Mrs. Smith, who shuddered at the bare idea of being touched by that creature.

"Through this act of impulsive pity he was brought back again within the pale of human relations with his new surroundings. He never forgot it—never.

"That very same morning old Mr. Swaffer (Smith's nearest neighbour) came over to give his advice, and ended by carrying him off. He stood, unsteady on his legs, meek, and caked over in half-dried mud, while the two men talked around him in an incomprehensible tongue. Mrs. Smith had refused to come downstairs till the madman was off the premises; Amy Foster, far from within the dark kitchen, watched through the open back-door; and he obeyed the signs that were made to him to the best of his ability. But Smith was full of mistrust. 'Mind, sir! It may be all his cunning,' he cried repeatedly in a tone of warning. When Mr. Swaffer started the mare, the deplorable being sitting humbly by his side, through weakness, nearly fell out over the back of the high two-wheeled cart. Swaffer took him straight home. And it is then that I come upon the scene.

"I was called in by the simple process of the old man beckoning to me with his forefinger over the gate of his house as I happened to be driving past. I got down, of course.

"'I've got something here,' he mumbled, leading the way to an outhouse at a little distance from his other farm-buildings.

"It was there that I saw him first, in a long, low room taken upon the space of that sort of coach-house. It was bare and whitewashed, with a small square aperture glazed with one cracked, dusty pane at its further end. He was lying on his back upon a straw pallet; they had given him a couple of horse-blankets, and he seemed to have spent the remainder of his strength in the exertion of cleaning himself. He was almost speechless; his quick breathing under the blankets pulled up to his chin, his glittering, restless black eyes reminded me of a wild bird caught in a snare. While I was examining him, old Swaffer stood silently by the door, passing the tips of his fingers along his shaven upper lip. I gave some directions, promised to send a bottle of medicine, and naturally made some inquiries.

"'Smith caught him in the stackyard at New Barns,' said the old chap in his deliberate, unmoved manner, and as if the other had been indeed a sort of wild animal. 'That's how I came by him. Quite a curiosity, isn't he? Now tell me, doctor—you've been all over the world—don't you think that's a bit of a Hindoo we've got hold of here?'

"I was greatly surprised. His long black hair scattered over the straw bolster contrasted with the olive pallor of his face. It occurred to me he might be a Basque. It didn't necessarily follow that he should understand Spanish; but I tried him with the few words I know, and also with some French. The whispered sounds I caught by bending my ear to his lips puzzled me utterly. That afternoon the young ladies from the Rectory (one of them read Goethe with a dictionary, and the other had struggled with Dante for years), coming to see Miss Swaffer, tried their German and Italian on him from the doorway. They retreated, just the least bit scared by the flood of passionate speech which, turning on his pallet, he let out at them. They admitted that the sound was pleasant, soft, musical—but, in conjunction with his looks perhaps, it was startling—so excitable, so utterly unlike anything one had ever heard. The village boys climbed up the bank to have a peep through the little square aperture. Everybody was wondering what Mr. Swaffer would do with him.

"He simply kept him.

"Swaffer would be called eccentric were he not so much respected. They will tell you that Mr. Swaffer sits up as late as ten o'clock at night to read books, and they will tell you also that he can write a cheque for two hundred pounds without thinking twice about it. He himself would tell you that the Swaffers had owned land between this and Darnford for these three hundred years. He must be eighty-five to-day, but he does not look a bit older than when I first came here. He is a great breeder of sheep, and deals extensively in cattle. He attends market days for miles around in every sort of weather, and drives sitting bowed low over the reins, his lank gray hair curling over the collar of his warm coat, and with a green plaid rug round his legs. The calmness of advanced age gives a solemnity to his manner. He is clean-shaved; his lips are thin and sensitive; something rigid and monachal in the set of his features lends a certain elevation to the character of his face. He has been known to drive miles in the rain to see a new kind of rose in somebody's garden, or a monstrous cabbage grown by a cottager. He loves to hear tell of or to be shown something what he calls 'outlandish.' Perhaps it was just that outlandishness of the man which influenced old Swaffer. Perhaps it was only an inexplicable caprice. All I know is that at the end of three weeks I caught sight of Smith's lunatic digging in Swaffer's kitchen garden. They had found out he could use a spade. He dug barefooted.

"His black hair flowed over his shoulders. I suppose it was Swaffer who had given him the striped old cotton shirt; but he wore still the national brown cloth trousers (in which he had been washed ashore) fitting to the leg almost like tights; was belted with a broad leathern belt studded with little brass discs; and had never yet ventured into the village. The land he looked upon seemed to him kept neatly, like the grounds round a landowner's house; the size of the cart-horses struck him with astonishment; the roads resembled garden walks, and the aspect of the people, especially on Sundays, spoke of opulence. He wondered what made them so hardhearted and their children so bold. He got his food at the back-door, carried it in both hands, carefully, to his outhouse, and, sitting alone on his pallet, would make the sign of the cross before he began. Beside the same pallet, kneeling in the early darkness of the short days, he recited aloud the Lord's Prayer before he slept. Whenever he saw old Swaffer he would bow with veneration from the waist, and stand erect while the old man, with his fingers over his upper lip, surveyed him silently. He bowed also to Miss Swaffer, who kept house frugally for her father—a broad-shouldered, big-boned woman of forty-five, with the pocket of her dress full of keys, and a gray, steady eye. She was Church—as people said (while her father was one of the trustees of the Baptist Chapel)—and wore a little steel cross at her waist. She dressed severely in black, in memory of one of the innumerable Bradleys of the neighbourhood, to whom she had been engaged some twenty-five years ago—a young farmer who broke his neck out hunting on the eve of the wedding-day. She had the unmoved countenance of the deaf, spoke very seldom, and her lips, thin like her father's, astonished one sometimes by a mysteriously ironic curl.

"These were the people to whom he owed allegiance, and an overwhelming loneliness seemed to fall from the leaden sky of that winter without sunshine. All the faces were sad. He could talk to no one, and had no hope of ever understanding anybody. It was as if these had been the faces of people from the other world—dead people—he used to tell me years afterwards. Upon my word, I wonder he did not go mad. He didn't know where he was. Somewhere very far from his mountains—somewhere over the water. Was this America, he wondered?

"If it hadn't been for the steel cross at Miss Swaffer's belt he would not, he confessed, have known whether he was in a Christian country at all. He used to cast stealthy glances at it, and feel comforted. There was nothing here the same as in his country! The earth and the water were different; there were no images of the Redeemer by the roadside. The very grass was different, and the trees. All the trees but the three old Norway pines on the bit of lawn before Swaffer's house, and these reminded him of his country. He had been detected once, after dusk, with his forehead against the trunk of one of them, sobbing, and talking to himself. They had been like brothers to him at that time, he affirmed. Everything else was strange. Conceive you the kind of an existence over-shadowed, oppressed, by the everyday material appearances, as if by the visions of a nightmare. At night, when he could not sleep, he kept on thinking of the girl who gave him the first piece of bread he had eaten in this foreign land. She had been neither fierce nor angry, nor frightened. Her face he remembered as the only comprehensible face amongst all these faces that were as closed, as mysterious, and as mute as the faces of the dead who are possessed of a knowledge beyond the comprehension of the living. I wondered whether the memory of her compassion prevented him from cutting his throat. But there! I suppose I am an old sentimentalist, and forget the instinctive love of life which it takes all the strength of an uncommon despair to overcome.

"He did the work which was given him with an intelligence which surprised old Swaffer. By-and-by it was discovered that he could help at the ploughing, could milk the cows, feed the bullocks in the cattleyard, and was of some use with the sheep. He began to pick up words, too, very fast; and suddenly, one fine morning in spring, he rescued from an untimely death a grand-child of old Swaffer.

"Swaffer's younger daughter is married to Wilcox, a solicitor and the Town Clerk of Colebrook. Regularly twice a year they come to stay with the old man for a few days. Their only child, a little girl not three years old at the time, ran out of the house alone in her little white pinafore, and, toddling across the grass of a terraced garden, pitched herself over a low wall head first into the horsepond in the yard below.

"Our man was out with the waggoner and the plough in the field nearest to the house, and as he was leading the team round to begin a fresh furrow, he saw, through the gap of a gate, what for anybody else would have been a mere flutter of something white. But he had straight-glancing, quick, far-reaching eyes, that only seemed to flinch and lose their amazing power before the immensity of the sea. He was barefooted, and looking as outlandish as the heart of Swaffer could desire. Leaving the horses on the turn, to the inexpressible disgust of the waggoner he bounded off, going over the ploughed ground in long leaps, and suddenly appeared before the mother, thrust the child into her arms, and strode away.

"The pond was not very deep; but still, if he had not had such good eyes, the child would have perished—miserably suffocated in the foot or so of sticky mud at the bottom. Old Swaffer walked out slowly into the field, waited till the plough came over to his side, had a good look at him, and without saying a word went back to the house. But from that time they laid out his meals on the kitchen table; and at first, Miss Swaffer, all in black and with an inscrutable face, would come and stand in the doorway of the living-room to see him make a big sign of the cross before he fell to. I believe that from that day, too, Swaffer began to pay him regular wages.

"I can't follow step by step his development. He cut his hair short, was seen in the village and along the road going to and fro to his work like any other man. Children ceased to shout after him. He became aware of social differences, but remained for a long time surprised at the bare poverty of the churches among so much wealth. He couldn't understand either why they were kept shut up on week-days. There was nothing to steal in them. Was it to keep people from praying too often? The rectory took much notice of him about that time, and I believe the young ladies attempted to prepare the ground for his conversion. They could not, however, break him of his habit of crossing himself, but he went so far as to take off the string with a couple of brass medals the size of a sixpence, a tiny metal cross, and a square sort of scapulary which he wore round his neck. He hung them on the wall by the side of his bed, and he was still to be heard every evening reciting the Lord's Prayer, in incomprehensible words and in a slow, fervent tone, as he had heard his old father do at the head of all the kneeling family, big and little, on every evening of his life. And though he wore corduroys at work, and a slop-made pepper-and-salt suit on Sundays, strangers would turn round to look after him on the road. His foreignness had a peculiar and indelible stamp. At last people became used to see him. But they never became used to him. His rapid, skimming walk; his swarthy complexion; his hat cocked on the left ear; his habit, on warm evenings, of wearing his coat over one shoulder, like a hussar's dolman; his manner of leaping over the stiles, not as a feat of agility, but in the ordinary course of progression—all these peculiarities were, as one may say, so many causes of scorn and offence to the inhabitants of the village. *They* wouldn't in their dinner hour lie flat on their backs on the grass to stare at the sky. Neither did they go about the fields screaming dismal tunes. Many times have I heard his high-pitched voice from behind the ridge of some sloping sheep-walk, a voice light and soaring, like a lark's, but with a melancholy human note, over our fields that hear only the song of birds. And I would be startled myself. Ah! He was different; innocent of heart, and full of good will, which nobody wanted, this castaway, that, like a man transplanted into another planet, was separated by an immense space from his past and by an immense ignorance from his future. His quick, fervent utterance positively shocked everybody. 'An excitable devil,' they called him. One evening, in the tap-room of the Coach and Horses, (having drunk some whisky), he upset them all by singing a love-song of his country. They hooted him down, and he was pained; but Preble, the lame wheelwright, and Vincent, the fat blacksmith, and the other notables, too, wanted to drink their evening beer in peace. On another occasion he tried to show them how to dance. The dust rose in clouds from the sanded floor; he leaped straight up amongst the deal tables, struck his heels together, squatted on one heel in front of old Preble, shooting out the other leg, uttered wild and exulting cries, jumped up to whirl on one foot, snapping his fingers above his head—and a strange carter who was having a drink in there began to swear, and cleared out with his half-pint in his hand into the bar. But when suddenly he sprang upon a table and continued to dance among the glasses, the landlord interfered. He didn't want any 'acrobat tricks in the tap-room.' They laid their hands on him. Having had a glass or two, Mr. Swaffer's foreigner tried to expostulate: was ejected forcibly: got a black eye.

"I believe he felt the hostility of his human surroundings. But he was tough—tough in spirit, too, as well as in body. Only the memory of the sea frightened him, with that vague terror that is left by a bad dream. His home was far away; and he did not want now to go to America. I had often explained to him that there is no place on earth where true gold can be found lying ready and to be got for the trouble of the picking up. How, then, he asked, could he ever return home with empty hands when there had been sold a cow, two ponies, and a bit of land to pay for his going? His eyes would fill with tears, and, averting them from the immense shimmer of the sea, he would throw himself face down on the grass. But sometimes, cocking his hat with a little conquering air, he would defy my wisdom. He had found his bit of true gold. That was Amy Foster's heart; which was 'a golden heart, and soft to people's misery,' he would say in the accents of overwhelming conviction.

"He was called Yanko. He had explained that this meant Little John; but as he would also repeat very often that he was a mountaineer (some word sounding in the dialect of his country like Goorall) he got it for his surname. And this is the only trace of him that the succeeding ages may find in the marriage register of the parish. There it stands—Yanko Goorall—in the rector's handwriting. The crooked cross made by the castaway, a cross whose tracing no doubt seemed to him the most solemn part of the whole ceremony, is all that remains now to perpetuate the memory of his name.

"His courtship had lasted some time—ever since he got his precarious footing in the community. It began by his buying for Amy Foster a green satin ribbon in Darnford. This was what you did in his country. You bought a ribbon at a Jew's stall on a fair-day. I don't suppose the girl knew what to do with it, but he seemed to think that his honourable intentions could not be mistaken.

"It was only when he declared his purpose to get married that I fully understood how, for a hundred futile and inappreciable reasons, how—shall I say odious?—he was to all the countryside. Every old woman in the village was up in arms. Smith, coming upon him near the farm, promised to break his head for him if he found him about again. But he twisted his little black moustache with such a bellicose air and rolled such big, black fierce eyes at Smith that this promise came to nothing. Smith, however, told the girl that she must be mad to take up with a man who was surely wrong in his head. All the same, when she heard him in the gloaming whistle from beyond the orchard a couple of bars of a weird and mournful tune, she would drop whatever she had in her hand—she would leave Mrs. Smith in the middle of a sentence—and she would run out to his call. Mrs. Smith called her a shameless hussy. She answered nothing. She said nothing at all to anybody, and went on her way as if she had been deaf. She and I alone in all the land, I fancy, could see his very real beauty. He was very good-looking, and most graceful in his bearing, with that something wild as of a woodland creature in his aspect. Her mother moaned over her dismally whenever the girl came to see her on her day out. The father was surly, but pretended not to know; and Mrs. Finn once told her plainly that 'this man, my dear, will do you some harm some day yet.' And so it went on. They could be seen on the roads, she tramping stolidly in her finery—gray dress, black feather, stout boots, prominent white cotton gloves that caught your eye a hundred yards away; and he, his coat slung picturesquely over one shoulder, pacing by her side, gallant of bearing and casting tender glances upon the girl with the golden heart. I wonder whether he saw how plain she was. Perhaps among types so different from what he had ever seen, he had not the power to judge; or perhaps he was seduced by the divine quality of her pity.

"Yanko was in great trouble meantime. In his country you get an old man for an ambassador in marriage affairs. He did not know how to proceed. However, one day in the midst of sheep in a field (he was now Swaffer's undershepherd with Foster) he took off his hat to the father and declared himself humbly. 'I daresay she's fool enough to marry you,' was all Foster said. 'And then,' he used to relate, 'he puts his hat on his head, looks black at me as if he wanted to cut my throat, whistles the dog, and off he goes, leaving me to do the work.' The Fosters, of course, didn't like to lose the wages the girl earned: Amy used to give all her money to her mother. But there was in Foster a very genuine aversion to that match. He contended that the fellow was very good with sheep, but was not fit for any girl to marry. For one thing, he used to go along the hedges muttering to himself like a dam' fool; and then, these foreigners behave very queerly to women sometimes. And perhaps he would want to carry her off somewhere—or run off himself. It was not safe. He preached it to his daughter that the fellow might ill-use her in some way. She made no answer. It was, they said in the village, as if the man had done something to her. People discussed the matter. It was quite an excitement, and the two went on 'walking out' together in the face of opposition. Then something unexpected happened.

"I don't know whether old Swaffer ever understood how much he was regarded in the light of a father by his foreign retainer. Anyway the relation was curiously feudal. So when Yanko asked formally for an interview—'and the Miss, too' (he called the severe, deaf Miss Swaffer simply *Miss*)—it was to obtain their permission to marry. Swaffer heard him unmoved, dismissed him by a nod, and then shouted the intelligence into Miss Swaffer's best ear. She showed no surprise, and only remarked grimly, in a veiled blank voice, 'He certainly won't get any other girl to marry him.'

"It is Miss Swaffer who has all the credit of the munificence: but in a very few days it came out that Mr. Swaffer had presented Yanko with a cottage (the cottage you've seen this morning) and something like an acre of ground— had made it over to him in absolute property. Wilcox expedited the deed, and I remember him telling me he had a great pleasure in making it ready. It recited: 'In consideration of saving the life of my beloved grandchild, Bertha Wilcox.'

146

"Of course, after that no power on earth could prevent them from getting married.

"Her infatuation endured. People saw her going out to meet him in the evening. She stared with unblinking, fascinated eyes up the road where he was expected to appear, walking freely, with a swing from the hip, and humming one of the love-tunes of his country. When the boy was born, he got elevated at the 'Coach and Horses,' essayed again a song and a dance, and was again ejected. People expressed their commiseration for a woman married to that Jack-in-the-box. He didn't care. There was a man now (he told me boastfully) to whom he could sing and talk in the language of his country, and show how to dance by-and-by.

"But I don't know. To me he appeared to have grown less springy of step, heavier in body, less keen of eye. Imagination, no doubt; but it seems to me now as if the net of fate had been drawn closer round him already.

"One day I met him on the footpath over the Talfourd Hill. He told me that 'women were funny.' I had heard already of domestic differences. People were saying that Amy Foster was beginning to find out what sort of man she had married. He looked upon the sea with indifferent, unseeing eyes. His wife had snatched the child out of his arms one day as he sat on the door-step crooning to it a song such as the mothers sing to babies in his mountains. She seemed to think he was doing it some harm. Women are funny. And she had objected to him praying aloud in the evening. Why? He expected the boy to repeat the prayer aloud after him by-and-by, as he used to do after his old father when he was a child—in his own country. And I discovered he longed for their boy to grow up so that he could have a man to talk with in that language that to our ears sounded so disturbing, so passionate, and so bizarre. Why his wife should dislike the idea he couldn't tell. But that would pass, he said. And tilting his head knowingly, he tapped his breastbone to indicate that she had a good heart: not hard, not fierce, open to compassion, charitable to the poor!

"I walked away thoughtfully; I wondered whether his difference, his strangeness, were not penetrating with repulsion that dull nature they had begun by irresistibly attracting. I wondered. . . ."

The Doctor came to the window and looked out at the frigid splendour of the sea, immense in the haze, as if enclosing all the earth with all the hearts lost among the passions of love and fear.

"Physiologically, now," he said, turning away abruptly, "it was possible. It was possible."

He remained silent. Then went on—

"At all events, the next time I saw him he was ill—lung trouble. He was tough, but I daresay he was not acclimatized as well as I had supposed. It was a bad winter; and, of course, these mountaineers do get fits of home sickness; and a state of depression would make him vulnerable. He was lying half dressed on a couch downstairs.

"A table covered with a dark oilcloth took up all the middle of the little room. There was a wicker cradle on the floor, a kettle spouting steam on the hob, and some child's linen lay drying on the fender. The room was warm, but the door opens right into the garden, as you noticed perhaps.

"He was very feverish, and kept on muttering to himself. She sat on a chair and looked at him fixedly across the table with her brown, blurred eyes. 'Why don't you have him upstairs?' I asked. With a start and a confused stammer she said, 'Oh! ah! I couldn't sit with him upstairs, sir.'

"I gave her certain directions; and going outside, I said again that he ought to be in bed upstairs. She wrung her hands. 'I couldn't. I couldn't. He keeps on saying something—I don't know what.' With the memory of all the talk against the man that had been dinned into her ears, I looked at her narrowly. I looked into her short-sighted eyes, at her dumb eyes that once in her life had seen an enticing shape, but seemed, staring at me, to see nothing at all now. But I saw she was uneasy.

"'What's the matter with him?' she asked in a sort of vacant trepidation. 'He doesn't look very ill. I never did see anybody look like this before. . . .'

"'Do you think,' I asked indignantly, 'he is shamming?'

"'I can't help it, sir,' she said, stolidly. And suddenly she clapped her hands and looked right and left. 'And there's the baby. I am so frightened. He wanted me just now to give him the baby. I can't understand what he says to it.'

"'Can't you ask a neighbour to come in to-night?' I asked.

"'Please, sir, nobody seems to care to come,' she muttered, dully resigned all at once.

"I impressed upon her the necessity of the greatest care, and then had to go. There was a good deal of sickness that winter. 'Oh, I hope he won't talk!' she exclaimed softly just as I was going away.

"I don't know how it is I did not see—but I didn't. And yet, turning in my trap, I saw her lingering before the door, very still, and as if meditating a flight up the miry road.

"Towards the night his fever increased.

"He tossed, moaned, and now and then muttered a complaint. And she

148

sat with the table between her and the couch, watching every movement and every sound, with the terror, the unreasonable terror, of that man she could not understand creeping over her. She had drawn the wicker cradle close to her feet. There was nothing in her now but the maternal instinct and that unaccountable fear.

"Suddenly coming to himself, parched, he demanded a drink of water. She did not move. She had not understood, though he may have thought he was speaking in English. He waited, looking at her, burning with fever, amazed at her silence and immobility, and then he shouted impatiently, 'Water! Give me water!'

"She jumped to her feet, snatched up the child, and stood still. He spoke to her, and his passionate remonstrances only increased her fear of that strange man. I believe he spoke to her for a long time, entreating, wondering, pleading, ordering, I suppose. She says she bore it as long as she could. And then a gust of rage came over him.

"He sat up and called out terribly one word—some word. Then he got up as though he hadn't been ill at all, she says. And as in fevered dismay, indignation, and wonder he tried to get to her round the table, she simply opened the door and ran out with the child in her arms. She heard him call twice after her down the road in a terrible voice—and fled. . . . Ah! but you should have seen stirring behind the dull, blurred glance of those eyes the spectre of the fear which had hunted her on that night three miles and a half to the door of Foster's cottage! I did the next day.

"And it was I who found him lying face down and his body in a puddle, just outside the little wicker-gate.

"I had been called out that night to an urgent case in the village, and on my way home at daybreak passed by the cottage. The door stood open. My man helped me to carry him in. We laid him on the couch. The lamp smoked, the fire was out, the chill of the stormy night oozed from the cheerless yellow paper on the wall. 'Amy!' I called aloud, and my voice seemed to lose itself in the emptiness of this tiny house as if I had cried in a desert. He opened his eyes. 'Gone!' he said, distinctly. 'I had only asked for water—only for a little water. . . .'

"He was muddy. I covered him up and stood waiting in silence, catching a painfully gasped word now and then. They were no longer in his own language. The fever had left him, taking with it the heat of life. And with his panting breast and lustrous eyes he reminded me again of a wild creature under the net; of a bird caught in a snare. She had left him. She had left him—

149

sick—helpless—thirsty. The spear of the hunter had entered his very soul. 'Why?' he cried, in the penetrating and indignant voice of a man calling to a responsible Maker. A gust of wind and a swish of rain answered.

"And as I turned away to shut the door he pronounced the word 'Merciful!' and expired.

"Eventually I certified heart-failure as the immediate cause of death. His heart must have indeed failed him, or else he might have stood this night of storm and exposure, too. I closed his eyes and drove away. Not very far from the cottage I met Foster walking sturdily between the dripping hedges with his collie at his heels.

"'Do you know where your daughter is?' I asked.

"'Don't I!' he cried. 'I am going to talk to him a bit. Frightening a poor woman like this.'

"'He won't frighten her any more,' I said. 'He is dead.'

"He struck with his stick at the mud.

"'And there's the child.'

"Then, after thinking deeply for a while—

"'I don't know that it isn't for the best.'

"That's what he said. And she says nothing at all now. Not a word of him. Never. Is his image as utterly gone from her mind as his lithe and striding figure, his carolling voice are gone from our fields? He is no longer before her eyes to excite her imagination into a passion of love or fear; and his memory seems to have vanished from her dull brain as a shadow passes away upon a white screen. She lives in the cottage and works for Miss Swaffer. She is Amy Foster for everybody, and the child is 'Amy Foster's boy.' She calls him Johnny—which means Little John.

"It is impossible to say whether this name recalls anything to her. Does she ever think of the past? I have seen her hanging over the boy's cot in a very passion of maternal tenderness. The little fellow was lying on his back, a little frightened at me, but very still, with his big black eyes, with his fluttered air of a bird in a snare. And looking at him I seemed to see again the other one—the father, cast out mysteriously by the sea to perish in the supreme disaster of loneliness and despair."

"Amy Foster" was first published in the Illustrated London News, *December 14–28, 1901; it was then published in the collection* Typhoon and Other Stories *(1903).*

AFTERWORD

BEEBAN KIDRON AND FRED SCHEPISI

The following is a telephone inteview given from London by Beeban Kidron to Australian writer/director Fred Schepisi in Melbourne, August 7, 1997, after the final editing of the moview had been completed.

Schepisi dropped out of Catholic school at age fourteen and literally worked his way up from messenger to become head of the television department of a Melbourne advertising agency. In 1966 he founded his own production company, The Film House, directing and producing such movies as The Devil's Playground *(1976) and* The Chant of Jimmy Blacksmith *(1978). This success paved the way for his first US feature,* Barbarosa *(1982), which led to such films as* Roxanne *(1987),* The Russia House *(1990), and* Six Degrees of Separation *(1993). He is attracted to stories which pit strong outsiders against small-minded establishments, and is familiar with Conrad's "Amy Foster"—all of which contributed to a lively and fascinating discussion.*

Amy Foster *premiered at the Toronto Film Festival in September 1997.*

Fred Schepisi: What made you want to do this film?

Beeban Kidron: I was interested in the idea of two outsiders meeting and identifying each other's true goodness witthout even a common language.

Yes, that connection is very strong in the film. Amy immediately perceives something which for her is linked with good things coming from the sea. She's able to see in him what the others can't. It is because she has a more pure eye.

Exactly. The film has a fierce romanticism. It speaks of a love which goes even beyond the object of love being present. Beyond death. It was this extremity that fascinated me.

151

Yanko is an immigrant but the locals don't even quite understand that he is a foreigner.

Well, at first they think he is an escaped lunatic. After all, this is the end of the earth; no one really passes through.

The only outsiders they know speak a different dialect in the English language.

Exactly.

The concept of somebody not talking English is really bizarre to them.

So the immediate assumption is that he's mad. It is not until he meets Swaffer, who suggests he might be a "bit of a hindu," and then Kennedy who tries speaking to him in other languages, that anyone even thinks of him that way. It's a question of class. The concept of foreigner can exist for these more educated people, not for the villagers.

What about Amy? I remember her as almost speechless in the book.

It was a very difficult role to play . . . indeed, to cast. Rachel came to see me, and I was on the phone when she walked in the room and I was talking to someone, and she had this quality of being quite separate. She was very, very bright, fiercely bright, we had a chat and said good-bye. I got back to London and was sort of overwhelmed by the stillness of her and I felt that that was what I wanted. I'm actually very pleased with her performance. I think she's stunning; you always want to know what she's thinking, whether or not she's speaking.

Amy as a character is a little mysterious, she has an inner life that is not wholly explained. She is central to the film, not simply a creature of somebody else's imagination and yet she says and does very little. It's an unbelievably hard undertaking for actor and director alike.

Well, the qualities that you're talking about definitely come across and that's important. Most directors would say you've got to aim for about 120 percent because you're only going to end up with 80 percent anyway.

What about Kennedy's attraction to Yanko? Was it an intellectual connection? Or were you thinking of anything else?

If you're asking about his sexuality, it wasn't specifically that Kennedy fancied him. I think that Kennedy is a smart man . . .

He's a smart man and a man with morals.

. . . with little outside of his medical practice to do, his social life is playing bad chess with Swaffer, who's probably the closest thing to a smart man in the village. For Kennedy it started as intrigue. I think that his love is that of teacher, then friend; it becomes familial, and may be ultimately sexual, but that concerned me less than the idea of a passionate friendship.

I felt it was on that level. I liked the pleasure and pride that Kennedy took in Yanko's wanting him to educate and influence his son, and how touching that was for Kennedy.

The thing is that Kennedy lost his own family and has been cut off from all his emotions. His own love couldn't sustain beyond death. So the original thought that I had about the love that knows no bounds was something that Kennedy had to be given permission to feel. In a sense that's what Kennedy learns to do. He learns to feel.

Interestingly enough, Kennedy is one of the things that changed most radically between the first version of the script that I read and the last. Because it was such a positive change it appeared seamless. I think one of the interesting things about adaptation in general is that you can make radical changes but if it is within the tone and spirit of the piece, it feels as though it was always there.

I assume that you were originally sent the script.

Yes.

Did you go back to the book to see what was perhaps missing in the translation?

Absolutely. In fact, when I first read the script I thought, "This is very interesting but not completely achieved," and given that it was based on Conrad's story, I assumed that all the missing links would be in the book. So I dashed out to buy the book and I realized what an extraordinary job Tim Willocks had done. The screenplay seemed to be much more complete than the book. The original story is twenty or thirty pages long and almost like a sketch. It's like an unfinished thought. Thematically it offers up most of what is in the film, but narratively it's not at all rich.

So what attracted the writer to it? Did he have the same kind of reason for doing the work as yourself?

I can't say specifically, but I know we share a fascination of Conrad's discourse on the treatment of strangers—what it is to be a stranger and what in each of us makes us strange. Because there is Yanko, a stranger/foreigner, but Amy is a stranger in her own place and in her own tongue. Perhaps we are all strangers to each other.

And was there the one writer all the way through the process?

Absolutely.

Well, that's an achievement in this day and age.

I think this constant changing of writers is a bad Hollywood habit. "Amy Foster" comes from Conrad, there is already a big voice there, and Tim had a very clear, passionate, and educated interpretation of that voice. I think whatever the limitations one individually possesses, the strength of his authorship needed to be protected. It was not a project that could afford a confused voice. The art of screenwriting often lies in the ability and willingness to rewrite. Again and again. For the story, the budget, the characters, the locations. He did that. Keeping the energy flowing is part of the director's job.

Can you think of a couple of things in the film that are a complete departure from the story?

Amy originally didn't do or have anything of her own, so it seemed as though she was going through the story as a vehicle for Yanko's love. The passivity was not working so I tried to imagine how we could understand her without her having to explain herself. What rare things does she have, what needs to be understood? The notion that she had a hidden world in which there was a different order gave birth to the idea of the cave, which is not in Conrad's story. Those scenes—the scene where they dance together and she shows him her treasures, the scene where they make love in the cave, the fire in the cave—were all things that I tried to use to make the audience participants; things that Yanko can imagine but we needed to see.

That's excellent, actually, and very strong in the film in helping to understand her.

In fact, another such scene is when Amy washes Yanko. I remember there was a moment when I said to Tim that we needed an act of religious kindness. You know, the kindness of Christians, an act so pure but that has a sensuality to it. That's how the woodshed scene was born. I hoped it would be a purification, like washing the feet of Christ. Tim wrote it and and I filmed it almost verbatim. For me it's one of the most successful scenes in the film—a scene with barely any words.

Obviously you considered the various choices about how to start the film, and you decided to begin it near the end of the story by introducing Amy Foster and her child right at the beginning. Was this to intrigue the audience and to add a tension and a question throughout the film about how it's going to end?

I suppose it's to do with setting the tone for the piece. It is outside of the traditional English sort of costume drama, a slightly poetic note.

Yes, it has a sort of romantic feel to it—gothic romantic.

I'm not entirely happy with the way the film begins. I love all that running up the mountain but then the way Kennedy comes into her sickroom and we start the tale is a bit awkward. Conrad spent a lot more time in the Ukraine explaining how the Ukrainians were duped into coming to America. Shipping agents had false telephone machines and pretended that the King of America could be contacted on it to invite the emigrants to America, to tell them the streets are paved with gold. So he spent a lot of time on the emigrant experience, which we didn't really have time for. In the first version of the script I read, there were twenty more minutes in the Ukraine before we even started the film.

I was responsible for cutting it and starting where we were going to end, on that mountainside. In retrospect, I think it doesn't help establish whose point of view the film truly is, is it Yanko's or Amy's or is it Yanko's and handed over to Amy? I'm not altogether sure that there wasn't another better place to start the film. That is one of the things that haunts me as a director. The making of a film is just one part of a film's importance in your life. There are the things that attracted you to it that begin way before the film existed. Then there is the film as it finally comes out, which is dependent on whether it was raining one day, or you ran out of light, or the studio wanted it that way and you lost the battle, or you simply fucked up because you had a headache. Any number of practical reasons. Then there's the film that you continue to make in your imagination, long after it's finished. I always feel a Woody Allen sort of panic, realizing that now that I have finished the film, I know the film I would like to make. And I can't work out whether that's my failing as a director or whether it is the very nature of the task to continue to...

... Well, I think it's pretty true that halfway through any film you've learnt a lot of things which you wish you could apply to the film but you can't be-

cause it doesn't apply to the film as it has been shot to that point; because of its style it's just not relevant. In fact, you would make a bad film if you applied these new lessons. You've already learnt and gone beyond it. So it's always going to be frustrating.

Did you rehearse with the actors?

Yes, I did. For a couple of weeks before shooting I always talk to the actors about where their characters come from and develop an agreed history. It's a way of getting to know them a bit. So you know what they might say when they're in trouble, and what they might respond to. Also, inevitably, there's never enough time on the day and it is so helpful to be able to use shorthand, to refer to an assumption between the two of you of an agreed character. So a lot of my rehearsal is one on one, and not so much about the scenes as about the history.

Do you find that in rehearsals, when you cast particular actors, that they bring qualities to the material that needs to be incorporated in the writing?

Yes. On this occasion I had such an astute group of actors, I found their contributions awe-inspiring. Ian McKellen's command of the English language is beyond that of any actor I know. Kathy Bates has an emotional directness that sometimes feels so much like a laser beam that you could get burnt. Rachel I have already talked about, and Vincent did such incredible work transforming himself from Swiss/Spanish to Ukrainian that on some days I would ask him to ad lib in Ukrainian, forgetting it wasn't his native tongue. It was one of the great pleasures of working back in Europe.

I always feel the actors are the "front line." I think that my job is to make them feel safe and stay focused. If you don't believe in the characters they create you're sunk. So you'd better be ready to give your right arm to get them there.

Do you think you came close to making the film you intended?

I intended to make one of those Sunday afternoon films that I used to watch on rainy days, the kind you never even knew the titles of. Often they were black and white, high drama/love stories where people love impossibly, under impossible circumstances, and they always had all those fantastic actors whom I can't name. I don't know whether there is room for a film of that nature in this harsh film market, but that was what I was trying to do. A high tragedy. I hope I made that.